WOMEN WHO Write

VOLUME II

by Lucinda Irwin Smith

JULIAN Ⓜ MESSNER
PUBLISHED BY SIMON & SCHUSTER
NEW YORK   LONDON   TORONTO   SYDNEY   TOKYO   SINGAPORE

ACKNOWLEDGMENTS

The author would like to thank the women writers who appear in this book for sharing their insights into a writer's life. I am grateful for their time and for their agreeing to be interviewed.

I would also like to thank Yvonne Lucas and my editor at Simon & Schuster, Adriane Ruggiero.

PHOTO ACKNOWLEDGMENTS

PEARL S. BUCK: The Bettmann Archive; ZORA NEALE HURSTON: Courtesy of the New York Public Library Picture Collection; GERTRUDE STEIN: The Bettmann Archive; MARY WOLLSTONECRAFT: The Bettmann Archive; MOURNING DOVE: Courtesy of Lucinda Irwin Smith; EDNA ST. VINCENT MILLAY: The Bettmann Archive; MURASAKI SHIKIBU: Giraudon/Art Resource, N.Y.; MAYA ANGELOU: Steve Dunwell; CHARLAYNE HUNTER-GAULT: Courtesy of the author; SUSAN ISAACS: Ingrid Estrada; KATHERINE VAZ: Grey Crawford; WENDY WASSERSTEIN: James Hamilton, courtesy of Royce Carlton; MARGARET ATWOOD: Barbara Nettleton; BEBE MOORE CAMPBELL: Gene Golden; DENISE CHÁVEZ: Georgia McInnis; NIEN CHENG: Courtesy of the author; ANNIE DILLARD: Bill Burkhart; RITA DOVE: Fred Viebahn; FANNIE FLAGG: Courtesy of T. J. Hartman Public Relations; PAULA GUNN ALLEN: Tama Rothschild; SUE GRAFTON: Nick Vaccaro; CHERYL MARIE WADE: Brenda Prager; FAY WELDON: Mark Gerson; SUSAN GRIFFIN: Irene Young; HISAYE YAMAMOTO: Marilyn Sanders; SUSAN CHEEVER: Jerry Bauer; LOUISE ERDRICH: Michael Dorris; MELISSA MATHISON: Dominick Conde/Star File, Inc.; CYNTHIA VOIGT: Courtesy of Scholastic, Inc.

JULIAN Ⓜ MESSNER
Published by Simon & Schuster, 1230 Avenue of the Americas, New York, New York 10020. Copyright © 1994 by Lucinda Irwin Smith. All rights reserved including the right of reproduction in whole or in part in any form. JULIAN MESSNER and colophon are trademarks of Simon & Schuster.
Book design by Anahid Hamparian.
Manufactured in the United States of America
10 9 8 7 6 5 4 3 2 1
Library of Congress Cataloging-in-Publication Data
(Revised for volume 2)
Smith, Lucinda. Women who write, volume II. Bibliography: p. Includes index. Discusses the nature and significance of authorship and uses interviews and biographical profiles to analyze the contributions of notable women writers. 1. Women and literature—United States. 2. Women and literature—Great Britain. 3. American literature—Women authors—History and criticism. 4. English literature—Women authors—History and criticism. 5. Women authors—Interviews. 6. Authorship. [1. Women authors, American. 2. Women authors, English. 3. Authors, American. 4. Authors, English. 5. Authorship] I. Title. PS147.s65 1994 810.9'9287 [920] 89-12290 ISBN 0-671-87253-2

FOR MALLORY

"I don't write out of what I know. It's what I don't know that stimulates me. I merely know enough to get started. Writing is discovery; it's talking deep within myself." [1]

—TONI MORRISON
WINNER OF THE 1993 NOBEL PRIZE FOR LITERATURE

CONTENTS

PREFACE

In *Women Who Write, Volume I* Joyce Carol Oates explains, "The serious writer is stubborn, single-minded, convinced of his ability to write . . . hence not much in need of advice."

The interviews on these pages do not necessarily offer advice. Instead, they explore with honesty and humor the personal and professional aspects of a writer's life.

I have always been inspired by writers discussing their craft, and in *Volume II*, I wanted to discover more about writers of the past and the present. When I was a student, I was introduced to the *Paris Review* series of interviews. These behind-the-scenes portraits left a lasting impression on me. Penetrating the private world of working writers seems to somehow enhance the totality of the artistic experience.

Women Who Write, Volumes I and *II* discuss writers from the past and present and link the heritage of women writers with the commonality of their struggle.

While these biographies and interviews provide insights into each writer's life and the creative process, this is only one part of the story. You must also read the poems, novels, plays, and other works written by these women.

It is your prerogative whether to heed the information on these pages as advice, encouragement, or as a warning. As Anne Tyler stated in *Volume I*, "I like the feeling writing gives me of entering other people's lives—lives I'd never otherwise have had the chance to live."

"On the following pages, you will have the opportunity to enter the lives of many different writers from the past and present. It is my hope the experience will prove enriching as you enter each new chapter of your writing life.

Lucinda Irwin Smith

INTRODUCTION

Writing a book is an eerie process. It's like solving a mystery. You start with nothing but a vague idea, an outline, a hunch. In both fiction and nonfiction, you chip away at words until a form slowly begins to emerge. This is a painstaking process that not only involves research and editing, but it also involves many hours of dreaming—the mind-work that pulls ideas out of a hazy landscape and into a plan.

When you begin, your mind visualizes the final book: You picture the handsome volume with your name printed prominently on the cover. You imagine the brilliant reviews and huge projected sales. While you indulge your fantasies, however, the stark blank page stares mockingly from your writing pad, typewriter, or computer screen. How and with what you are going to fill your blank page remains unknown.

In the beginning, the task of writing a book seems overwhelming. You know you have several hundred blank pages in need of words. You assemble your empty files, thick stacks of yellow pads, long pencils with intact erasers, and other pristine supplies. You close your eyes and imagine that somewhere in the universe of knowledge, you'll locate the thousands of words that will fill your book. You project a year or more into the future and *know* that it will happen. The files will be filled, the pencils will be sharpened into oblivion, and the supplies will be consumed.

When I began planning this second volume of *Women Who*

Write, I too faced the blank page. Armed with my equipment, I had the daunting task of locating and then interviewing a diverse group of contemporary writers. Of the forty writers I approached, twenty-two said yes. This response obviously reinforced my notion that an essential part of the artistic process is analyzation and discussion. Many writers seem to enjoy, and in fact are challenged by, sharing and examining the secrets of their craft.

Throughout history, the lives of writers and the details of their artistic processes have been found to be as compelling as their work. An eager audience of other writers, scholars, and literary devotees wants to learn more about the people whose office is their mind.

As several of the writers explain in their interviews, writing is like having a spirit take permanent possession of their being. The spirit is both an unshakable tormentor and a nurturing friend.

The completion of any project brings a mixed bag of relief and uneasiness. A writer must put away her prizes, replenish her supplies, and jump back into the unknown.

As I stack my bulging files into several storage boxes and place my dog-eared research books back on the shelf—thus clearing the canvas for a new project—I am renewed by the experience of writing this book and by the insights I have obtained from these interviews. They will continue to inspire, confuse, and encourage me as I solve one puzzle and begin another. I'm hopeful this book will, likewise, serve as a companion for you, the writer, each time you enter the maze and begin the process of writing.

ON CREATIVITY AND WRITING

"The creative instinct is, in its final analysis and in its simplest terms, an enormous extra vitality, a super-energy, born inexplicably in an individual, a vitality great beyond all the needs of one's own living—an energy which no single life can consume. This energy consumes itself then in creating more life, in the form of music, painting, writing, or whatever is its most natural medium of expression." [1]

—Pearl S. Buck

Creativity. To define it seems almost to contradict it. Although one hesitates to dissect this word, one wonders if creativity must be defined in order for it to be realized.

What comes into your mind when you consider creativity? Do you think of words such as "original," "free," "expansive," "new," "unique," or "unlimited?"

Under the synonyms for "creative," *Roget's Thesaurus* lists the word "godlike." Is the act of creation so powerful that each time we create something, we tap into the "god" or essence of our being? Do our humble innovations make us godlike each time we take dabs of paint and transform them into an image or each time we link unrelated words into an essay, poem, or novel? If this is the case, it's no wonder creativity can be somewhat frightening.

The concept of creativity suggests a vast spectrum of abilities. At its highest level, creativity can be associated with the works of Michelangelo and Shakespeare. Creativity, however, is not only about creating masterpieces or changing the world with revolutionary medical, scientific, or political theories. Creativity can also manifest itself through fundamental and everyday tasks such as cooking, arranging flowers in a vase, and getting dressed for work. Creativity is the means by which people express their uniqueness. Obviously, some people have great gifts or talents that reveal themselves through the arts or other fields specifically designated as creative. Everyday life, however, provides unlimited possibilities for all people to express creativity in tasks both great and small.

All creative endeavors involve the same essential element, however. Whether you're writing a novel or preparing a meal, each act requires some degree of *courage*.

To develop an artistic ability such as writing, a person needs creative courage, and this involves taking risks. Creative courage is the courage to reach into the unknown or unexplored areas of your self and risk uncovering things that might be painful. It's the courage to confront the truth. Creative courage is ignoring the nagging voice in your subconscious that says, "You'll never do it. Take the easy way instead." It's the courage to move from thought to action. And it's the courage to present your ideas and work before others.

While everyone has the capacity for creativity, not everyone has the courage. The people who do push ahead are often those whose drive proves greater than their fear. Overcoming fear is the greatest obstacle to creativity. In his book *Free Play: Improvisation in Life and Art,* Dr. Stephen Nachmanovitch states: "What we have to express is already with us, *is* us, so the work of creativity is not a matter of making the material come, but of unblocking the obstacles to its natural flow." [2]

Indeed, the desire to create is an integral part of our nature. Obstacles are everywhere if we choose to stumble over them. When people are truly inspired, their passion forces them around the barriers, and they get the story out. Obstacles can be found in the environment, among one's peers, friends, and family. Throughout history, society has attempted to suppress creativity because it can be threatening to the status quo.

Creativity is an abstract concept that requires real tools for expression. It's one thing to hear a symphony in your head, but if you don't have the technical skills to write it down or play it on a musical instrument, what good is it? As Nachmanovitch explains, "To create, we need both technique and freedom from technique." [3]

A person needs to practice the skills of her art so that the technique fades into the background, and the art, music, dance, or literary work can surface. Truly creative people do not just sit around and create. They work hard. The obsession to expel the music, novel, or painting that haunts them, makes it compulsory that they master their medium. A writer who isn't disciplined enough to work on her craft, is a writer who is frustrated. No creative person can achieve any peace when she's unable to express herself. You must take a risk and find out if you have the ability. Then once you gain the needed skills, you must tell your story and risk exposing new and equally complicated demons. Hence, the double-edged sword of creativity.

Because "art" presupposes a unique and original entity, an artistic work seems to defy any rules or conventions that take away from the purity of its creation. And yet writers or individuals who aspire to express themselves through the arts, must overcome any resistance to form and structure. While these boundaries may seem to contradict creativity, they are necessary to translate and communicate an abstraction.

Dr. Rollo May, the renowned psychoanalyst, explains this conflict in his book *The Courage to Create:* "Creativity arises out of the tension between spontaneity and limitations, the latter (like the river banks) forcing the spontaneity into the various forms which are essential to the work of art or poem. Form provides the essential boundaries and structure for the creative act." [4]

For a writer, words are the limitations that express the unlimited. The biographies and interviews on the following pages reveal the battle that is waged and the fears that are overcome to put one's thoughts onto a page. A writer brings experience and perception to the creation of new life in words. To transcend one's existence and touch the spark of something intangible—something beyond death—is to grasp the ultimate freedom. Creative courage enables us to search for who we are, and then go beyond.

"I am a writer who came of a sheltered life. A sheltered life can be a daring life as well. For all serious daring starts from within." [5]
                                                                    —Eudora Welty

ON WOMEN AND WRITING

"Outwardly, what is simpler than to write books? Outwardly, what obstacles are there for a woman rather than for a man? Inwardly, I think the case is very different; she still has many ghosts to fight, many prejudices to overcome. Indeed it will be a long time still, I think, before a woman can sit down to write a book without finding a phantom to be slain, a rock to be dashed against." [1]

—Virginia Woolf, "Professions for Women"

If you were to begin writing a novel today, what would you write about? Would the main character of your book, if she were a woman, be concerned with professional goals, romantic pursuits, combating social injustice, the relationship with her family, or driving a dogsled across Alaska?

Why are the interests of women labeled "female," while the concerns of men considered the concerns of everyone? All writers, in fact all human beings, are the product of their historical environment. If a person is born female, obviously she has a different perspective on her existence than a man. Likewise, two people born in different countries or from different generations will view the world differently.

Somehow the "female perspective" has been twisted around to have negative connotations.

In Virginia Woolf's essay, "Professions for Women," she also presents the concept of "killing the angel in the house." The "angel" is always hovering over the shoulder of the woman writer, encouraging her to be nice, to be pure, and to be nurturing. Before the writer is able to write, however, she must murder the angel.

Women today are still haunted by these angels and/or demons. Women must exorcise age-old preconceptions about their gender. Women are still attempting to prove themselves. Although women may suffer from some of the old phantoms, there are always new and deceptive undertones lurking in this era of "equality."

Hopefully, the day will come when the unique perspective women have, precisely because of their sex, will not be regarded as an outsider's advantage. Women will win prestigious honors without the rejoinder, "It's about time."

Women must write the truth, uninfluenced by any past ghosts or present obligatory voices. This is not to deny one's nature. While women must celebrate their history and the accomplishments of the feminist movement, there will be no real gains unless women writers are first recognized for their abilities as individuals.

INTRODUCTION
TO WRITERS
OF THE PAST

We live in an era of sensationalism and celebrity. The media relentlessly exposes the "truth" about a person's life in the belief that the more sordid a person's background is, the more appealing she becomes to a mass audience. A person has a much better chance at immortality if scandal and intrigue dominate her days rather than ordinary, productive endeavors.

Many writers have been pushed into posthumous fame because their suicides or their romantic pursuits grabbed the imagination of the public. The work of a writer will often be obscured behind the more riveting drama of her life.

Critics argue that a person's art should be viewed separately from her life. They claim too much importance is placed on biography, and an inordinate amount of energy is spent attempting to make connections between a person's life and her work. In actuality, a reader doesn't need to know a single detail about a writer—perhaps not even her name—in order to appreciate her work.

As one studies women writers and their history, however, it becomes immediately apparent that the combination of life and art enhances an individual's work. One woman's passion to tell her story, the sacrifices she makes and the ramifications of this dedication are revealed through the chronicle of a person's life. Without biography, the artistic development of these courageous women writers of the past could not be appreciated.

The women profiled in this section were chosen at random. Some of them are famous, while others are more obscure. The women were selected from a wide range of time periods and cultural backgrounds. All have different writing styles. These women represent an enormous diversity in where and how they lived and in the paths they took to realize their creative goals. Each of these writers was a strong and independent woman.

There is a common thread of political activism in the lives of Mary Wollstonecraft, Edna St. Vincent Millay, Pearl S. Buck, and Mourning Dove. They were not only dedicated to a particular cause, but they also used their writing to change attitudes and heighten public awareness. Both Mary Wollstonecraft and Murasaki Shikibu had daughters who became successful writers. Zora Neale Hurston and Mourning Dove were storytellers who transcribed the folklore of their Southern and Native American cultures, respectively. Gertrude Stein and Zora Neale Hurston represent opposite extremes of a writer's life. Gertrude Stein lived a comfortable, artistic life. Her writing was the perfect accompaniment to a rich, rewarding existence. Zora Neale Hurston represents an artist who made great sacrifices to write and consequently could not achieve a balance in her life and work. Because she chose to put her art on a higher level of importance than the everyday pleasures of life, generations will forever enjoy the amazing tales written by this remarkable woman.

If one could conduct a posthumous interview with each of

these writers, what questions would one ask? It is an interesting exercise to imagine all the questions and then go in search of the answers. The study of a writer's life allows one to discover the multifaceted dimensions of an individual and the world in which she lived.

As a result of the trials, adventures, joys, and sorrows of these very real individuals, we are richer for both their lives and for their art.

PEARL S. BUCK

"It is the highest reward when a writer hears that a book, written in doubt and solitude, has reached a human heart with a deeper meaning than even the writer had been aware of, as she wrote. It is the something extra, the unexpected return." [1]

$\mathcal{P}$EARL S. BUCK did indeed receive the highest reward when, in 1938, she won the Nobel Prize for literature. During her career, she wrote more than sixty books and 200 magazine articles.

Pearl Comfort Sydenstricker Buck was born June 26, 1892, in Hillsboro, West Virginia. Soon after her birth, the family returned to China where Pearl's father, Absalom Sydenstricker, was a Presbyterian minister and missionary. Her mother, Caroline, was a devoted wife who followed her husband into the remotest provinces of China so that he could convert the Chinese people to Christianity. Because of the harsh circumstances in which they lived, the Sydenstrickers lost four of their seven children to illness. They were also forced to move many times because of war and uprisings directed at white foreigners.

Pearl S. Buck learned to speak Chinese before she spoke English. Her nurse, Wang Amah, taught her the language and filled her young mind with colorful and magical stories of the Chinese people. Buck read profusely as a child and had a profound curiousity about people. Her mother was a strict tutor who taught Pearl grammar and introduced her to the English classics.

In 1905, Buck attended Miss Jewell's boarding school in Shanghai, and in 1910 she returned to the United States to enter Randolph–Macon Woman's College in Lynchburg, Virginia. She began writing very seriously and several of her stories were published.

Although Buck taught briefly in the United States, she returned to China to care for her ailing mother. Three years later, she married John Lossing Buck, an American agricultural expert who worked with the Presbyterian mission board.

When the Bucks returned to the United States in search of medical treatment for their disabled daughter, Buck realized that in addition to providing great pleasure, writing could also be a source of much needed income. While in the United States, she published several articles and also obtained a master's degree in English literature from Cornell University.

In 1930, Buck published her first novel, *East Wind: West Wind,* and in 1931, at the age of forty, Buck published *The Good Earth,* her most famous work.

In 1932, *The Good Earth* won the Pulitzer Prize. Six years later Buck was awarded the Nobel Prize for this novel and for the biographies of her parents, *The Exile* and *Fighting Angel.*

The joy Pearl S. Buck felt in receiving this great honor was somewhat diminished by the controversy that immediately followed. Although many critics claimed her work wasn't literary enough to win such a distinguished prize, the true hostility was directed at Buck because she was a woman. The critics felt the prize should have been awarded to a man.

Buck was always sensitive to this double standard. "Women artists in any field are not taken as seriously as men, however serious their work. It is true that they often achieve high popular success, but this counts against them as artists." [2]

The press continued its criticism of Buck, and despite having won the Nobel Prize, she adopted a male pseudonym for several of her novels. She took the name "John Sedges" in much the same way that George Sand and George Eliot took pseudonyms decades before. "I chose the name of John Sedges, a simple one, and masculine because men have fewer handicaps in our society than women have in writing, as well as in other professions." [3]

In addition to her large body of work, Pearl S. Buck is also remembered for her humanitarian efforts. She founded the East–West Association to promote better relations between diverse regions of the world. She also founded Welcome House and the Pearl S. Buck Foundation, which provided adoptive families for unwanted children. Buck herself adopted eight children.

In 1934, Buck separated from her husband, John, and soon after married Richard Walsh, the president of the John Day Publishing Company, the publishing house that had published all of her work.

Pearl S. Buck continued writing novels about China, including *Dragon Seed, The Pavilion of Women,* and *The Promise,* as well as three volumes of autobiography. She died in 1973 at the age of eighty-one in Danby, Vermont.

ZORA NEALE HURSTON

"The force from somewhere in space which commands you to write in the first place, gives you no choice. You take up the pen when you are told and write what is commanded. There is no agony like bearing an untold story inside you." [1]

The life of Zora Neale Hurston radiates with intensity and tragedy. She gave herself up to the creative urgency within her and was consequently directed by passion rather than practicality. Her life is an example of living for the moment, and her journey seems a storyteller's dream come true. Yet behind the legend of this woman, is a grim, unhappy ending. She died alone, sick, and destitute.

Zora Neale Hurston was born on January 7, 1901, in a very unusual American town. Eatonville, Florida, was incorporated in 1886 as an all-black township. This unique environment provided a relatively safe haven from prejudice, and it also offered a rich heritage of black folklore and culture.

Hurston's mother, Lucy Potts Hurston, married at fourteen and gave birth to eight children. Zora's father, John Hurston, was a restless man who was a Baptist preacher and three-time mayor of Eatonville. Lucy died when Zora was nine, but she instilled in her daughter the challenge to "jump at de sun." [2]

The early security of Zora Neale Hurston's life crumbled when her mother died. At the age of fourteen Zora took her first step down a long, uncertain road. She worked as a maid and wardrobe girl for a traveling dramatic troupe. She then took a job as a waitress and enrolled in Morgan Academy in Baltimore. At Morgan Academy, she first read Samuel Taylor Coleridge's "Kubla Khan," which sparked a fascination with the magic of words. She made a vow, "This is my world, I said to myself, and I shall be in it and surrounded by it, if it is the last thing I do on God's green dirt-ball."[3]

Zora next attended Howard University in Washington, D.C. While at Howard, she joined the literary club and published her first short story. Barnard College in New York then awarded Hurston a scholarship in 1926, and she went on to receive her B.A. degree in anthropology.

Hurston continued her studies in anthropology at Columbia University, and because of encouragement from Dr. Franz Boas, she returned to Eatonville to research its folklore. Her book *Mules and Men* was based on this research. It was published in 1935.

Borrowing two dollars for postage, Hurston sent off the manuscript of her novel *Jonah's Gourd Vine* to a publisher. It was accepted the same day she was evicted from her home.

Zora Neale Hurston's financial struggles paralleled her growing success and recognition as a writer. She held many jobs and late in her career was discovered working as a maid. Although she claimed she was doing research on a story, the truth was that Hurston was always teetering on the edge of poverty.

Zora Neale Hurston received a great deal of criticism for her portrayal of black people. Many people felt her stories about the rural South stereotyped blacks and therefore encouraged racism. During the 1930s and 1940s, there was a movement to remove certain images from African–American history. Hurston saw the value of one's cultural roots, however, and celebrated the diversity of all Americans.

In 1937, Zora Neale Hurston wrote her masterpiece, *Their Eyes Are Watching God,* while on a Guggenheim Fellowship in the Caribbean. This work was followed by her autobiography, *Dust Tracks on a Road.* Her last book, *Seraph on the Swanee,* was published in 1948. During her thirty-year career as a writer, the largest royalty Hurston ever received was $900.

In 1948, Hurston was arrested on a morals charge in New York City, and although the charge was dismissed, the experience pushed Zora further into self-imposed isolation. For the next years, she worked as a reporter, teacher, and librarian. She lived in a series of tiny cabin-like homes with only the barest essentials. She used orange crates for chairs and had a small kerosene stove for cooking. Despite these hardships, she continued to write, and she published several essays and magazine articles.

Zora Neale Hurston suffered a stroke in October 1959 and entered the St. Lucie County (Florida) welfare home where she died on January 28, 1960. Although more than a hundred people attended her funeral, there wasn't enough money for a gravestone.

Hurston's burial site remained unmarked and overgrown with weeds for thirteen years. In 1973, Alice Walker, the Pulitzer Prize-winning author, made a pilgrimage to the Garden of Heavenly Rest. She searched through waist-high weeds and found the unmarked plot. Walker then made arrangements for a simple stone to be placed above the grave. It reads:

Zora Neale Hurston, "A Genius of the South," 1901-1960, Novelist, Folklorist, Anthropologist.

GERTRUDE STEIN

*G*ERTRUDE STEIN considered question marks "revolting" and the use of commas "positively degrading."[1] Stein reinvented language and challenged classical ideas about sentence structure. She pushed the boundaries of what was considered acceptable in much the same way that artists such as Pablo Picasso and Georges Braque revolutionized form and shape and brought into question long-held theories about art.

Gertrude Stein first became famous as a patron of the arts, then as a personality, and finally as a writer. She longed for fame and yearned to be recognized for her literary genius. Although her writings were recognized as truly original and innovative by intellectuals and other writers, it was not until she was sixty years old that Stein achieved popular recognition. The publication of *The Autobiography of Alice B. Toklas* not only made Stein a celebrity, but it also made her wealthy.

Gertrude Stein was born on February 3, 1874, in Allegheny, Pennsylvania. Her parents, Daniel and Amelia, were Jewish immigrants from Germany. Gertrude was the youngest of five children. When they were children, Gertrude formed an almost inseparable bond with her brother Leo, who was the youngest son. The family moved to Vienna and then to Paris. When Gertrude was five years old, the Steins returned to the United States and settled in Oakland, California. Gertrude was only fourteen when her mother died, and she was seventeen when she lost her father. Gertrude's eldest brother, Michael, moved the family to San Francisco. He wisely invested his father's money and provided an income for the siblings for the rest of their lives.

Although Gertrude Stein never received a high school diploma, in 1892 she followed her brother Leo to Boston where he was studying at Harvard. She enrolled as a special student at Radcliffe College. At Radcliffe, Stein studied under the famous psychologist and philosopher William James. His ideas greatly influenced her writing. Gertrude studied medicine at Johns Hopkins University for two years. When Leo moved to Europe, however, she abandoned her plans to become a psychologist and followed him. In 1903, they took an apartment together at 27, rue de Fleurus in Paris.

The early 1900s was an exciting time to be in Paris. Leo and Gertrude Stein spent a portion of their small income on the paintings of several young, unknown artists who were attempting to move art in a new, modern direction. Within a few years, their collection included works by Paul Cézanne, Pierre-Auguste Renoir, Paul Gauguin, Henri Matisse, and Pablo Picasso.

In addition to a passionate interest in art, Stein had committed herself to becoming a serious writer and having her work published. In 1909, she finished a collection of stories entitled *Three Lives*. In *Three Lives*, Gertrude Stein introduced a device known as the "continuous present." This process used the repetition of speech to reveal the character's personality. By repeating something over and over again in a character's dialogue, she exposed different facets of the person's nature and challenged the concept of time and reality. Perhaps Stein's most famous repetitious phrase was, "Rose is a rose is a rose is a rose."[2]

Pablo Picasso was a frequent visitor to the Stein apartment. He painted Gertrude's portrait while working on *Les Demoiselles d'Avignon,* one of the pieces that ushered in the revolutionary movement known as cubism. This concept, like Stein's writing, repeated an image, and presented it from several perspectives. Leo Stein did not appreciate his sister's writing or Picasso's art. He moved out of the apartment, and the differences between the once inseparable brother and sister continued to grow. Their split coincided with Gertrude Stein's meeting Alice B. Toklas, who would become Gertrude's lifelong partner and companion. Alice took on the job of arranging Stein's schedule, organizing their house, and typing Gertrude's handwritten manuscripts.

During the 1920s, Paris was filled with American writers and intellectuals. Many writers visited Alice B. Toklas and Gertrude Stein in their salon, including Ernest Hemingway, Sherwood Anderson, Ezra Pound, and F. Scott Fitzgerald. Through the influence of these writers and other notable people, Stein began to acquire a following for her unique work. When she sent her book *The Making of Americans* to the publisher, he complained about the odd grammar. Stein ordered him not to change anything. Although she published *Tender Buttons* and *Geography and Plays* with a publishing house specializing in "new books for exotic tastes," it wasn't until *The Autobiography of Alice B. Toklas* that Stein achieved true celebrity.

Gertrude Stein toured America at the age of sixty and gave lectures at many universities. She greatly enjoyed the opportunity of returning to her homeland as a celebrity. During World War II, Stein stayed in the French countryside and became a favorite of American GIs who called her "Gertie." Stein died at the age of seventy-two on July 27, 1946. Alice B. Toklas lived another twenty-one years and was eventually buried beside Gertrude in Paris. On her deathbed, Gertrude asked Alice, "What is the answer?" When Alice failed to reply, Gertrude asked, "In that case, what is the question?" [3]

MARY WOLLSTONECRAFT

*T*hroughout the centuries, many courageous women have spoken out against injustice. One of these pioneers lived 200 years ago. When Mary Wollstonecraft wrote *A Vindication of the Rights of Woman,* she was presenting ideas that were truly revolutionary. "I here throw down my gauntlet, and deny the existence of sexual virtues, not excepting modesty. For man and woman, truth, if I understand the meaning of the word, must be the same. . . . Women, I allow, may have different duties to fulfill; but they are *human* duties, and the principles that should regulate them, I sturdily maintain, must be the same. To become respectable, the exercise of their understanding is necessary; there is no other foundation for independence of character."[1]

Mary Wollstonecraft witnessed the injustice against women firsthand in her home. The power in her writing comes from a great anger and frustration she developed in her early years. Soured by debt and poverty, Mary's father drank and relentlessly abused his wife. Unable to stop this tragedy, Mary became increasingly aware of women's powerlessness against men. She made it her purpose to educate women and encourage them to develop strength and self-reliance and fight for their rights.

Mary Wollstonecraft was the second of five children born to Edward John Wollstonecraft and Elizabeth Dickson on April 27, 1759. Although Edward inherited a substantial amount of money, he squandered it on poor investments. As their predicament worsened, so too did Edward's railings against his wife. Occasionally, Mary would sleep on the landing outside her mother's bedroom in a vain attempt to protect her.

One of Mary Wollstonecraft's closest friends and influential figures in her life was Fanny Blood. She came from similar family circumstances that included a harsh, overbearing father. Wollstonecraft was a devoted friend and traveled to be with Fanny in Portugal for the birth of her child. She arrived too late, for Fanny had already died in childbirth.

Another incident reveals Wollstonecraft's loyalty and abhorrence of abusive men. She intervened in her sister's intolerable marriage and literally removed Eliza from her husband's house. This was a very brave and somewhat scandalous act at the time, but it illustrates Mary's determination to never again be a passive bystander.

In 1787, Mary Wollstonecraft began putting her ideas on paper. Her first published work was a collection of essays about child raising entitled *Thoughts on the Education of Daughters*. Convinced that writing was indeed her calling, Wollstonecraft set out for London to live alone. She earned her living writing essays for the *Analytical Review* and translating German novels into English. When Wollstonecraft was twenty-eight, she published her first novel, *Mary*. A children's book, *Original Stories*, was published in 1789. The second edition of this book was illustrated by the poet and artist William Blake. In 1790, she wrote *A Vindication of the Rights of Man* as a response to the French Revolution. Her most famous book, *A Vindication of the Rights of Woman*, was published in 1792. She lashed out against the frivolity of women and criticized society for demeaning their role. She encouraged women to take responsibility for their lives. "It is time to effect a revolution in female manners—time to restore to them their lost dignity—and make them, as part of the human species, labour by reforming themselves, to reform the world."[2]

The ideals Mary Wollstonecraft spoke of in her book and hoped all women would achieve were in great contrast with the tragic reality of her own life. She left England after a failed romance and moved to France where she intended to personally document the French Revolution. There she fell in love with an American, Gilbert Imlay, and had a child she named Fanny. Mary's relationship with Imlay was stormy, and when she discovered his unfaithfulness, she tried to throw herself off a bridge. Despite the lack of any personal security, Wollstonecraft remained focused on her work and continued to write.

She returned to London determined to start a new life. In 1797, Wollstonecraft married the renowned philosopher and novelist William Godwin. She had finally found a relationship with happiness, love, and respect, but unfortunately, she died shortly after the birth of her daughter, Mary. Following the death of his wife, Godwin published her *Posthumous Works,* which contained Mary Wollstonecraft's love letters to Imlay. These letters caused a major scandal, and consequently her work was ignored for more than a century.

Although the public may have shunned the work of Mary Wollstonecraft, her daughter Mary Godwin was greatly influenced by the books of both her mother and father. She was known to sit on her mother's grave and read. At the age of seventeen, Mary married the great romantic poet Percy Bysshe Shelley, and two years later she wrote the legendary Gothic tale *Frankenstein.*

MOURNING DOVE

"I was born in a canoe on the Kootenai River, near Booner's Ferry, Idaho, in the Moon of the Leaves (April) 1888. My parents were traveling with a packtrain, which my uncle, Louie Stuikin, operated between Walla Walla, Washington, and Fort Steele, British Columbia, during the mining rush that year. My mother and grandmother were being ferried across the river when I arrived. The Indian who was paddling their canoe stripped off his shirt and handed it to grandmother, who wrapped me up in it." [1]

These are the words of Mourning Dove, the first Native American woman to write and publish a novel. She was born Christine Quintasket and was a member of the Okanogan tribe and the Colville reservation in the state of Washington. Her pen name was Mourning Dove or Humishuma.

Mourning Dove's father, Joseph Quintasket, or Dark Cloud, and her mother, Lucy Stuikin, were married in a log church built by missionaries.

Mourning Dove aspired to become a writer when she was very young. She briefly attended the Sacred Heart Convent in Ward, Washington. She left the school, however, because the nuns insisted she speak English instead of her native language, Salish. She later returned to the convent school and stayed for several more years. In 1913 she enrolled in the

Calgary Business School in order to perfect her English and learn to type.

Mourning Dove began working on her novel *Cogewea the Half Blood: A Depiction of the Great Montana Cattle Range* in 1912. In 1914, she met Lucullus Virgil McWhorter, a business-man who was interested in Indian culture. He offered to assist her with her novel while she devoted her energies to collecting folklore. In her forward to *Coyote Stories,* Mourning Dove speaks of her debt to McWhorter, the "blue eyed" Indian. She traveled throughout the Northwest and gathered the stories that would appear in *Coyote Stories.* The book was published in 1933.

The stories in this collection focus on the antics of Coyote, an Animal Person. "The Animal People were here first—before there were any real people. Our name for the Animal People is *Chip-chap-tiqulk.* . . . To the younger generations, *Chip-chap-tiqulk* are improbable stories; that is a result of the white man's schools. But to the old Indians, *Chip-chap-tiqulk* are not at all improbable; they are accounts of what really happened when the world was very young."[2]

Coyote was one of the most important Animal People. He was a lovable character whose pride prevented him from being any more than a prankster and rebel. In many of the tales, Coyote transforms himself into other animals in order to accomplish his mischievous escapades.

Mourning Dove was briefly married to a Flathead Indian named Hector McLeod in 1909. In 1919, she married Fred Galler, a Wenatchi. They were employed as migrant workers picking apples for ten hours a day. They were paid $1.50 per day. Exhausted, Mourning Dove would return home, pull out her antiquated typewriter and work on her novel.

Cogewea was not published until 1927. The publisher, Four Seas in Boston, insisted Mourning Dove pay part of the costs. Determined to see her work in print, Mourning Dove worked more hours to raise the money.

Mourning Dove was also a political activist, and she helped found the Colville Indian Association. In 1935, she became the first woman elected to the Colville Tribal Council. In addition to her work on behalf of Native causes, Mourning Dove spent the last years of her life writing her autobiography. The strain took a toll on her health, and she died on August 8, 1936. The official cause of death was recorded as "exhaustion from manic psychosis."

Known primarily as a storyteller, Mourning Dove learned many of the legends from her mother and grandmother (named *Soma-how-atqhu* or She-got-her-power-from-the-water), and added tales from other members of her tribe. Storytelling is the most personal method of capturing and sharing history. As Chief Standing Bear explains in the foreward to *Coyote Stories:* "We who lived the days of tribal life before our destruction began remember with gratefulness our storytellers and the delight and joy and richness which they imparted to our lives. We never tired of their tales, though told countless times. They will, forsooth, never grow old, for they have within them the essence of things that cannot grow old. These legends are of America, as are its mountains, rivers, and forests, and as are its people. They belong!"[3]

EDNA ST. VINCENT MILLAY

ords such as intoxicating, cynical, liberated, fiery, and rebellious were used to describe Edna St. Vincent Millay. She was *the* poet of the Jazz Age—a time when women's hemlines rose and feminine restraint was considered boring. If Edna St. Vincent Millay was the spokeswoman for the Roaring Twenties, she was also its most gifted and famous poet. Her legendary red hair and green eyes helped make her the darling of both intellectuals and bohemians.

Known simply as "Vincent" to her family, Edna St. Vincent Millay was born in Rockland, Maine, on February 22, 1892. Her father was a school superintendent who enjoyed gambling. He deserted his wife and three daughters when Millay was only twelve. Left on her own, Cora Millay supported her children as a practical nurse. She stressed the importance of education and encouraged her daughters to read. Edna not only loved literature, she also developed an appreciation of music and became an accomplished pianist. She briefly considered a career in music, but her devotion to writing prevailed.

At the encouragement of her mother, Edna St. Vincent Millay began writing when she was a young girl. During her freshman year in high school, she published her first poem in *St. Nicholas,* a literary magazine for young people. She signed her work "Vincent Millay."

In 1912, Millay entered her poem "Renascence" in a contest held by the journal the *Lyric Year.* Although the poem did not win, it received a great deal of attention and is still considered one of her finest poems. The poem was published in the journal and came to the attention of a prominent woman, Caroline Dow, who helped raise money for Edna's college education. At the age of twenty-one, Millay entered Barnard College and later in the year began her studies at Vassar.

Following graduation from Vassar, Edna St. Vincent Millay moved to Greenwich Village where she surrounded herself with artists and writers and began living a bohemian life. Pressed by financial need, she wrote magazine articles using the pseudonym "Nancy Boyd." Millay also wrote several plays and performed them with the Provincetown Players. One of the productions was an allegorical antiwar play, *Aria da Capo.*

The publication of Millay's first volume, *Renascence and Other Poems,* made her something of an instant celebrity. As her reputation grew, young women began memorizing her poems. Her words captured the passion, humor, and cynicism of her generation. In 1921, Millay gained national celebrity with the publication of two more volumes of poetry, *Second April* and *A Few Figs From Thistles.* Her poetry contained what was then considered to be a flippant attitude about love and responsibility. It prompted sharp criticism and was thought to be scandalous by some critics. The majority of her work was well received, however, and in 1923 another volume of verse, *The Harp-Weaver,* won the Pulitzer Prize.

Millay was known for her outspoken stand concerning causes in which she believed. She considered herself a feminist and became involved in many issues associated with women's rights. In 1923, she married Eugen Jan Boissevain, the widower of another well-known feminist, Inez Milholland. In keeping with her nonconformist nature, Edna and her husband chose to live in a three-story house that was 9 1/2 feet wide. It was the smallest house in Greenwich Village.

Despite her tendency to be rebellious in most areas of her life, Millay selected a conservative and yet challenging structure for her verse. She wrote primarily in the sonnet form, rather than in a more experimental style.

Some critics argued that Millay's involvement with politics harmed her creative output. She could not remain silent, however, when she witnessed injustice. In 1927, Millay's social conscience was roused by the Sacco and Vanzetti case. The plight of these Italian immigrants gained international attention. They were found guilty of murder and executed. Millay marched in protest, but to no avail. The supporters of Sacco and Vanzetti believed the men received an unfair trial because of their radical political beliefs. Millay voiced her outrage through articles, poetry, and a play.

In an attempt to find solitude from the demands of her career, Edna and her husband purchased a farm in upstate New York. They named their retreat "Steepletop" and spent extended periods of time there, away from the New York City literary scene. To ensure their isolation, they even had the farm's telephone removed.

During World War II, Millay once again used her poetry to speak out against injustice. In 1944 her poem "Poem and Prayer for an Invading Army" was broadcast on D-Day, as the Allied troops were landing at Normandy, France.

After the war, Millay refocused on her writing. Before she could finish a new volume, however, her husband suddenly became ill and died. Eugen had been Millay's constant and almost sole companion. She never recovered from his loss and found she could not tolerate the loneliness. Edna St. Vincent Millay died on October 19, 1950, in Austerlitz, New York, a little more than a year after the death of her husband.

MURASAKI SHIKIBU

"The Emperor and Her Majesty sat in their respective cur-
tained daises. They were as resplendent as the morning
sun, dazzling in their brilliance. The Emperor wore ordi-
nary court dress with wide trousers drawn in at the ankles.
Her Majesty wore her usual unlined crimson dress. . . .
Her mantle was of light purple figured silk. . . . The pat-
tern and colors were most unusual and up-to-date. Feeling
rather exposed out in front, I sat in the back, making
myself as inconspicuous as possible." [1]

This quotation is an entry in the diary of Murasaki
Shikibu, a Japanese court lady who lived more than
900 years ago. In addition to her richly detailed diary,
Murasaki also wrote a set of poetic memoirs and a novel entitled *The Tale of Genji.* Her diaries and poetic memoirs provide
a fascinating glimpse into the isolated world of medieval
Japanese royalty and the position of women in early Japanese
society. Murasaki's diary also reveals an honest and introspec-
tive look into the life of a woman and a writer.

Murasaki Shikibu was born around 973 or 975 A.D. While a
member of the court of Emperor Ichijō and Empress Shōshi,
Murasaki kept a diary in which she described in vivid detail
the lifestyle of Japan's aristocracy. Hers is an eyewitness
account of the elaborate and lengthy ceremonies that preoc-
cupied the members of the royal court.

Murasaki was raised in a rich, literary environment. Her great-grandfather was a poet and a scholar. He was involved in the completion of the first imperial anthology, the *Kokinshū*. Fifty-seven of his poems were published in various anthologies. Murasaki's grandfather and father were also poets and scholars. Additionally, Murasaki's father, Tametoki, served in a variety of bureaucratic positions. He was dedicated to education and passed on a love of verse to his son and daughter. However, Tametoki shared his society's attitude about women and education. Murasaki recounts a story in her diary that illustrates this attitude. It seemed that Murasaki was more adept than her brother in their lessons and often helped him when he made mistakes. Whenever her father witnessed such an exchange, he would say, "If only you were a boy, how proud and happy I should be."[2]

Murasaki explained that although young Japanese boys were not encouraged to read, it was considered even more inappropriate for young women to be educated. As a result, Murasaki was forced to conceal her knowledge and abilities.

Murasaki often traveled with her father to the various provinces where he served as governor. Tametoki spent his last years as a Buddhist priest.

In 998, Murasaki married Fujiwara no Nobutaka, governor of the province of Yamashiro. He was twice her age and had several wives. Their daughter was born in 999, and Nobutaka died two years later. After her husband's death, Murasaki began writing her novel *The Tale of Genji*. Her talent was noticed by the royal court, and she was asked to become one of the ladies-in-waiting to the empress.

Murasaki was primarily a companion and tutor to Empress Shōshi. As a lady-in-waiting, Murasaki had few responsibilities at court and was thus able to observe relationships among the courtiers and the other ladies-in-waiting. In her diary, she described in detail the elaborate rituals of court life. Murasaki also displayed a great sensitivity for nature, and her diary often mentions the moon, snow, and the change of seasons. She disapproved of gossip and shared her insight into making a success in the world of society. Although she never remarried, her diary hints that Murasaki was the concubine of a powerful man named Michinaga. He was the prime minister and the father of the empress.

When Emperor Ichijō died in 1011, his wife moved to a smaller palace. Murasaki followed and remained in the service of the empress. Murasaki died in 1015.

Murasaki's daughter, Echigo no Ben, or Kenshi, also served at court. She became a wet nurse to the future Emperor Goreizei. The role of wet nurse was to breast feed the infant. To be the imperial wet nurse was not only a great honor in medieval Japanese society, it was considered a position of great power. Kenshi married and had one son. She lived until the age of eighty-four. She was also a poet, and thirty-seven of her verses were included in the imperial anthologies.

The diary of Lady Murasaki Shikibu is not a dull, day-to-day record of routine events. Rather, it is a very personal and honest critique of a woman's life. The author's self-analysis is very contemporary in tone, and it seems as if it could have been written today. In her diary, Murasaki described the ideal etiquette for a woman: "The key to everything is to be pleasant, gentle, properly relaxed, and self-possessed; this is what makes for charm and composure in a woman. No matter how amorous or capricious one may be, as long as you are well-meaning at heart and refrain from anything that might cause embarrassment to others, you will be forgiven."[3]

INTRODUCTION
TO
CONTEMPORARY
WRITERS

*T*he twenty-two interviews on the following pages represent the enormous diversity of contemporary women writers. The writers that appear in these interviews are from many different areas: They live in England and Canada, and throughout the United States in such states as New York, New Mexico, Connecticut, Maryland, Wyoming, California, North Carolina, and Virginia. Their diversity is not limited to the region where they live. This remarkable group of women represents a wide range of ages, ethnic backgrounds, and education. These women writers work in many genres. They write autobiographies, biographies, short stories, newspaper articles, essays, novels, poems, plays, performance pieces, young adult novels, screenplays, and mysteries. Many of the writers work in more than several different formats.

Three of the writers interviewed for this book have won Pulitzer Prizes, and many have received other prestigious honors. While the majority of these women are well-known and have large followings, there are also writers who are appreciated by a smaller, yet growing, number of readers.

Although the writers themselves may be diverse, many

of their concerns are similar. Writing may be regarded as spiritual, adventurous, difficult, or pleasurable, but it is almost always viewed as an all-consuming job.

The interviews discuss the process, the environment, and the equipment, as well as the rewards and the sacrifices of writing. Some of the interviews are humorous, while others are very serious.

The changing roles of women, the responsibility of women writers, the history of women, and the method of developing women characters in fiction—all of these aspects are discussed in the interviews.

The majority of the interviews were conducted over the telephone. The other writers answered their questions by mail. The telephone interviews seemed more like dialogues than merely exchanges of questions and answers. "Why do you write?" was the first question asked of each writer.

The reader will discover that these writers did not achieve their success by accident. The message is clear: Writing is hard work. These writers are linked to the writers of the past by a passion and a commitment to their craft. The writers of the past were strong women who integrated their work with their other responsibilities and interests. The contemporary women writers also lead full and demanding lives. They raise children, become involved in political causes, and teach. Although some may lament the struggle, somehow the desire to write proves greater than any distraction found in the daily routine of life.

As Maya Angelou explains in her interview: "The more serious the writer—and that is to say if a person really wants to claim being a writer and consider that writing is their main, central, and most focused work—then it's very painful to write. It's very hard to write. It takes everything to write well."

The following interviews provide an honest and very personal look into the *everything* that constitutes a writer's life.

MAYA ANGELOU

MAYA ANGELOU was born in St. Louis, Missouri, and was raised in Stamps, Arkansas. She is the author of *I Know Why the Caged Bird Sings, Gather Together in My Name, The Heart of a Woman, All God's Children Need Traveling Shoes,* and *I Wouldn't Take Nothing for My Journey Now.* She is also the author of five collections of poetry, including: *Just Give Me A Cool Drink of Water 'fore I Diiie; Oh Pray My Wings Are Gonna Fit Me Well; And Still I Rise; Shaker, Why Don't You Sing?;* and *I Shall Not Be Moved.* Angelou read her poem "On the Pulse of Morning" at the inauguration of President Bill Clinton. She has written for television and film and has received numerous honorary degrees. Currently, Angelou is Reynolds Professor at Wake Forest University in Winston–Salem, North Carolina.

Why do you write?
MA: (laughter) Next question! I write because I love language, and I find it a wonderful conveyance to send my thoughts, or to gather my thoughts, and then to share them.

Is writing autobiography painful or freeing?
MA: A little of both. Probably, it's very painful, but it costs

to write anything. The more serious the writer—and that is to say if a person really wants to claim being a writer and consider that writing is their main, central, and most focused work—then it's very painful to write. It's very hard to write. It takes everything to write well. Nathaniel Hawthorne said, "Easy reading is damned hard writing." Just to write anything—not only autobiographical material, but to write an essay on spring—is very difficult. And I suppose it is freeing. I've never quite agreed with those who say that autobiographical writing is cathartic. I've not found that to be so. Each time a writer finishes a piece of work and has done it as well as she or he can do it, then one is a little freed.

Writing an autobiography is different than writing in a diary because you intend your thoughts to be read. Does that make you self-conscious with your life?
MA: No. I try not to be self-conscious. If I'm self-conscious about any of my work then I can't get into it sufficiently. Everyone is self-conscious to a degree, but the writer tries to contrive a kind of trance-like condition so she or he can get away from one's own self. If a person is writing a poem or a journalistic account of an event which has taken place, there is a certain amount of self-consciousness in it because you are there. You're the person with the pen or the typewriter or the computer or the word processor. So there is a certain amount of self-consciousness, but I try to entrance myself away from that.

I've read that you play solitaire as part of your writing process. Would you describe your writing environment?
MA: I keep a hotel room in my town, and I go there about

5:30 in the morning. I'm there until about midday. I have everything taken off the walls—all the photographs and paintings and little "home sweet home" samplers. I keep a Bible, a dictionary, Roget's Thesaurus, and a deck of cards in the room.

How does playing solitaire help you write?
MA: My grandmother used to make a statement when people said something she didn't think much of. She'd say, "I won't even put that on my little mind." I knew then that there was a large mind and a small mind. If I can engage my small mind with trivia, then I'm able to get past it and go to the large mind.

Do you feel that generally, young African-Americans have only a vague awareness of the struggle of their ancestors?
MA: Not quite. I see a much better, or a closer, observation that young men and women are having now vis-à-vis their history and their present.

Do you think young people are more in touch with their past?
MA: Yes, I do.

Is this also true for women?
MA: Absolutely. No one can say where she or he is going if a person doesn't know where they've been.

The title of one of your books is **I Know Why The Caged Bird Sings.** *How does that metaphor apply to persecuted people today? Why does the caged bird sing?*
MA: It's not just persecuted people, but everyone. Everyone is encaged. The line comes from a great poem by Paul Laurence Dunbar called "Sympathy." It's true of all human beings. I have a poem in my book *Shaker, Why Don't*

You Sing? called "Caged Bird," which I just recorded with Branford Marsalis. Frederick Douglass said, "The person who is struck must herself give the first cry." The person who knows the feeling must speak for themselves. That's true for the caged bird. The caged bird is the one who must sing; the one who must sing or die.

What message did you hope to convey to young people in your inaugural poem "On the Pulse of Morning?"
MA: We live in a wonderful country which is rich in wonders and rich in potential. Many of us are different, and we should have the attitude *vive la différence.* Different doesn't mean better or worse. It means more enriching.

You often stress the importance of friendship. Could you elaborate on this and how it relates to young people today?
MA: Everyone needs to have a friend, a brother, or a sister. Everyone needs someone who is courageous enough to tell a strong person that she or he hasn't quite made it. Everyone needs someone to tell them she or he hasn't done the best thing or acted in the best way. Everyone also needs someone to tell them they *have* acted in the best way and to compliment and commend them.

In this era of visual bombardment, do you think the written word still has the same power?
MA: Although it doesn't have the same power, it still has a power. I don't know what the same is. Young people have the television do a lot of their imagining for them, and that's rather sad. But television is also good, and I don't want to complain. I do know that when a person reads, she or he has the responsibility of creating the moving figures and the trees and whatever is described on the page.

Reading involves a person much more than watching television. The lyrics in songs, the lyrics in poetry, and the prose in a well-turned essay or phrase still have the power to move us to tears or to laughter.

CHARLAYNE HUNTER-GAULT

C HARLAYNE HUNTER-GAULT was born in Due West, South Carolina. She is the author of *In My Place,* an autobiography that recounts her experience as one of two students who first desegregated the University of Georgia in 1961. Charlayne Hunter-Gault is national correspondent for PBS's MacNeil/Lehrer NewsHour. She is the winner of two Emmy Awards and a Peabody Award. In 1988, Hunter-Gault returned to the University of Georgia where she became the first African-American to deliver the graduation address in the school's 203-year history. Hunter-Gault is the mother of two children.

Why do you write, or more specifically, why did you write your book?
CHG: Although I had been pursued for a long time by a variety of publishers to write this book about my life, I did not feel I had the distance. In 1988, I was invited back to the University of Georgia to give the graduation address. I had been the first black woman to graduate, and I was the first black person ever asked to give the graduation address. It was almost like a full circle of history. It seemed to be the right moment. An excerpt of the graduation speech was published in the *New York Times,* and the

publisher at Farrar Straus Giroux called me. He had been one of the people trying to get me to do the book. He said, "Okay, it's really time." And I said, "Okay, I agree with you." A lot of things came together. The first editor I ever had as a professional was William Shawn at the *New Yorker.* Since he was at the time consulting with Farrar Straus Giroux, I said that if he could edit the book, that would be the one thing that would push me over the edge. I saw that as another full-circle closing. The publisher agreed immediately. I wrote the book out of a sense of this historical circle closing. I also felt the time had come for those of us who had had certain experiences in the civil rights movement to begin singing our own song. There were very few books written by the actual participants. The majority of people who had written about the civil rights movement had been observers. And while many of the books are passionate and good, I believe we also need to tell our own stories because they are quite different. I had always thought Calvin Trillin did such a good job with his book *An Education in Georgia,* and how he told the story of desegregation. I thought, "There's nothing else for me to say," but in fact there was a lot more to write about. I had a very different perspective, especially about the things that had prepared me for that event. In the end, that's why I was propelled into writing this book.

In your book, you explain that you were inspired by the comic strip reporter Brenda Starr. Were there any other role models?
CHG: When I was growing up, there were not many women, and possibly no African-Americans, working in mainstream media. There were certainly not any on television or in the newspaper. My role models weren't people who were actually in journalism, but people like my grandmother who was an

avid newsperson. She read three newspapers a day and kept up with current events. There were no practitioners I could emulate, so I guess it was the stuff of dreams and fantasies that encouraged me. I have to say, I think my own life has turned out if not as, then perhaps even more, exciting than that of Brenda Starr.

I don't think she would argue with you.
CHG: We would probably have some long tales to tell one another.

What traits in your personality made journalism the ideal profession for you?
CHG: In the prologue to my book, I quote from Zora Neale Hurston's *Their Eyes Are Watching God:* "She had been getting ready for her great journey to the horizons in search of people; it was important to all the world that she should find them and they find her." I think this is part of the reason I went into journalism. My natural inclination is toward people. I come from a very people-oriented family. They were ministers and preachers. They were people in the center of life and activity. I was always interested in people and in their stories. I also have a highly energetic nature. I don't like to sit still. I don't like sitting behind a desk. I like to get out in the world. I was blessed with an understanding of my nature. I knew from a very early age that I had to do something that would allow me to get out and not be confined. As I matured, I began to see the potential for journalism as a weapon against injustice and human indignity. That was another part of the reason why journalism seemed to fit so well with my personality and values.

Does a journalist also need traits such as aggressiveness and determination?

CHG: I wouldn't say aggressive because that word has taken on a somewhat negative meaning. Rather than aggressive, it's having the will to want to get things done. It's wanting to change things and have people informed so they can make good decisions for themselves and for society. I think you have to be determined, as we say in the movement, "not to let nobody turn you 'roun.'" You must have a goal and not let anyone stand in the way of it. Sometimes that can be more than a notion, and sometimes that can create unrealistic expectations. I think there's a danger in that. The idea that you can, like the Army says, "Be all that you can be," is a great goal. An important first step is having the confidence that you can do it. Confidence and self-esteem are both important. You need to have a belief in yourself. This belief will help when you run into obstacles on your way to realizing your goal. Some people may never realize their ultimate goal, but if they are confident about themselves and their ability, they will be better prepared to deal with whatever develops. The most desirable frame of mind is to be strong, know where you want to go, and use everything you have to get there.

You talk about the importance of solitude in your book. Why is it important for journalists, or writers, or for that matter anyone, to have solitary moments?

CHG: No matter where you live, whether it's in a hustle-bustle city like New York or a smaller place, things can have a way of crowding in on you. Because journalists are in a position of trying to take complex things and simplify them, it's essential to step back from the hustle and bustle and look at what it is you're doing, as well as how and why you're doing it. That's another one of those ideals or goals which is not always easy to attain. Again, this was one of the reasons I wanted to write my book. By having the distance, stepping back, and not rushing into it, I was able to get a better perspective. That perspective helped me write a more honest book. We try to write, or to record, what H.L. Mencken called, "The rough draft of history." And even though it is a rough draft, you want it to be as accurate as possible. In the kind of journalism I've always done, I try and put things into context. Nothing happens in isolation or in a vacuum, and yet so much of the news is reported in that way. It's no wonder people are not as informed as they might be. They're not getting good information. It's important to not only preserve your sanity, and not to get too caught up, but also to preserve a special eye on what's happening.

Are you ever intimidated by the people you interview either because they're famous or because they might be hostile toward you?
CHG: No. I think it has something to do with the way I was brought up. My father was particularly strong. He was a person who took on the world. As I indicated in the book, he prepared me to do the same thing. I went into this work pretty much unintimidated by most things. Also, when I went into the University of Georgia, I was in this special environment, and I was often at the center of news. While this may have also been a reason, I think it's primarily the way I was raised. I was taught that I should respect people and that people should respect me.

Does it take a certain amount of courage to be a journalist? Would you say you either have it or you don't?

CHG: No. I think you develop it. Most of us evolve as we go through our lives and careers, and we probably get stronger. I've seen people who were once very intimidated—people who were not very aggressive or forceful—learn how to do it. Even though I was brought up not to be intimidated by people, I think the more I have traveled and the more people I have dealt with, the stronger I have become. Not that I was ever intimidated, but I feel I've become stronger and stronger. The more people you deal with, the easier it is. I'm not saying you have to start out that way, or that it's something innate. For example, a person can learn to write. You can learn the craft by working at it, by writing a lot, by getting good advice, and by getting a good editor. Everyone needs an editor, no matter how good a writer you are. There are many things that can be learned. If you don't like people and you're not curious, it's pretty hard to develop these traits. Some of the other things, however, can come with practice, work, and exposure.

Is your desire to tell the story one of the reasons you push yourself past the grim realities you are frequently forced to confront as a journalist?

CHG: Someone has to be the conduit through which information is conveyed. I see myself as that conduit. There is an audience that cannot be in the places I am. When I was in Somalia, I thought it was very important to try and do the kind of reporting that would bring people as close as possible to the experience I was having. I approached it in a different way from other stories. It was a very emotional, wrenching kind of story. I think people were interested in what was happening there, and yet most of what they were seeing had been visceral. I wanted to try and put some of that in perspective. You have to bear in mind why you do what you do and for whom. That helps you keep your own emotions in check even if you might have an emotional reaction to some of the more difficult kinds of stories I report.

How does your strong religious faith affect your work? I under-stand how it can help, but does it ever hinder you in any way in terms of being objective?
CHG: No, I don't think so. Religious faith gives you a belief in yourself and makes you strong enough to take on some of the more difficult challenges. It's a very positive thing. It is a way of enabling you to do what you have to do. From time to time you have to deal with stories that are dangerous and difficult. I don't think you can be effective if you are so afraid of what might happen that you can't go out and do the story. I don't think you have to be a cowboy necessarily, but prudence, care, and good judgment are all important, especially when you're in dangerous circumstances. Faith plays a role in that.

Can young journalists aspire to help stop the violence through their access to world conflicts?
CHG: I don't think that is the journalist's role. If you're an advocate, and there is room for advocacy, then you can cer-tainly do whatever you think is important to help stop the violence. In the main, however, most journalists aren't there to help stop the violence, but to tell the story and to get the information to the public. Then it becomes a matter of the public will to do what it thinks is important along with the policymakers. But my premise is always that I don't need to be an activist. It is my responsibility to inform the public so they have the kind of information that will help them make good decisions and exercise good judgment in whatever

actions they take. I don't see my role as one aimed at stopping the violence, but rather as one that influences the public to act in one way or another, depending upon how well informed they are.

How do you relax? How do you get away from everything?
CHG: I'm not sure I ever really relax. If your beat, as it were, is the world, you always want to stay informed. I'm very uncomfortable when I've been out of the news loop for a while. I don't know that getting away is a luxury I ever totally enjoy. I ski, I play tennis, I exercise, and from time to time I get away. I think all of those things are important to help put some balance in life. Balance is important. As long as I had small children, I automatically had balance. The one thing I have learned in this business is that when you do have the opportunity to relax, you learn to relax totally, intensely. It's an intense business, so you relax intensely when that moment comes. I can get more out of a day than a lot of people can get out of a week.

Do you have any advice for young journalists in terms of their personal lives?
CHG: Balance in one's life is very important. You should try and have something other than your career as a major factor in your life. Your career is important, but I think a career is enhanced if you have a broader perspective on where it fits in. I have always found that having a family added a very important dimension to my existence. Having a loving family helps cushion a lot of the inevitable disappointments and frustrations. If your work is your only source of reward or punishment, then that's a very limiting environment. If you have a life that is as well rounded as possible, then you can give a lot to your work and career. I think you can give even

more when you have that kind of support from outside your career. Young people should look for support systems. Whether it's at church, within women's groups, or within groups with male or female interests, everyone needs a place where they can go and talk about the inevitable frustrations. We're not a perfect society yet. Chances are, we'll always be striving toward it rather than reaching it. Life is evolving. Life is never static. Coping with change can be quite challenging. It's very helpful if you have someone or ones with whom you can share your experiences.

SUSAN ISAACS

SUSAN ISAACS was born in Brooklyn, New York, and attended Queens College. One of her first writing jobs was as senior editor for *Seventeen* magazine. She has also written articles for other magazines, as well as political speeches. Isaacs is the author of several novels including: *Compromising Positions, Shining Through, Magic Hour, Close Relations, Almost Paradise,* and *After All These Years.* She has also written the screenplays for *Compromising Positions* and *Hello Again.* She is married to Elkan Abramowitz, a trial lawyer, and is the mother of two children. Isaacs lives on Long Island, New York.

Why do you write?
SI: I had a story to tell, and nobody else would write it for me. Also, my need to tell that story was enormous.

How did you begin writing? Did you keep a diary as a child?
SI: No. I wasn't one of those sensitive flowers who kept a journal. Although I could always write a simple declarative sentence that stood up to a teacher's scrutiny, it never occurred to me to write for a living. Writing was just something I did easily, the way musical people can carry a tune. I fell into writing after college. At that time, I didn't know what to do with my life; no one had asked me to marry them. In 1966, I went to an employment agency and took a test to be a computer programmer. It sounded like an interesting field. Unfortunately, I flunked the test. The

employment counselor said there was an opening at *Seventeen* magazine. I said it sounded frivolous. She said that was all they had, so I took the job. That's how I became a writer. Two years later, when I filled out a passport application, I put "writer" on the line marked "occupation." I was a little taken aback when I saw that, but I was also very pleased that that's what I was.

Why do you think it's difficult for women to regard their writing as their profession?

SI: Some women can't acknowledge that they're indeed professional writers rather than dabblers or housewives who happen to have a certain talent. There are very few men—in fact I can't think of any—who would hesitate and ask themselves, "Am I really a writer?" the way women do. And do you know anyone who would dare ask a male novelist about his "hobby"—writing?

Is this the result of conditioning?

SI: Yes. That's all it is. It's because of conditioning that some women cannot think of themselves as professionals, as full-fledged adults when you come down to it. They don't want to take credit for their talent and for how strong and hardworking they really are. Successful writers are damn tough, and tough isn't feminine. But this attitude is changing.

Writers and other creative people sometimes feel a little guilty because they are doing what other people think they want to do.

SI: It intrigues me that so many people really yearn to write, who in fact *burn* to do it, yet are so poor at it when they try. You hear them describe what they're writing, and you think, "Wow, I'd love to read that." Then when you read it, it's perfectly dreadful. My guess is, a writer's particular style or voice is something she is either born with or has developed by the time she's seven. Although many people may have this gift, they can never be sure until they actually attempt to write a novel. I suppose that's why people have such difficulty writing at the beginning; writing that first work that so desperately wants to be written. Do they have literary talent or just literary desire? That can be very scary. It's much more pleasant to be a potentially great novelist than actually to be one who isn't even mediocre. Also, people who go from fiction workshop to fiction workshop, refining the same forty pages, aren't novelists. To be one, you have to complete the work, and that takes guts, energy, and enormous effort.

So at this stage of your life you feel you've earned the right to call yourself a novelist?

SI: Yes, I really feel I have. Yet ideally, all my efforts should never be seen by the reader. It may be that the narrator is truly one of the author's voices; that each narrator is some facet of Susan Isaacs; but in my books the reader should not know that the omniscient narrator is this dame on Long Island sitting at a computer. A novelist is a god creating a universe, and god should be unknowable and invisible. Obviously, the reader knows I've written the book, but I shouldn't intrude as a personality. I shouldn't be there.

You mentioned that writing is hard. Has success made writing easier, or harder, or different in any way?

SI: It's gotten easier because I'm more sure of myself. I'm also not afraid my talent is going to disappear. I don't worry too much that if I go away for Memorial Day, I may not be a writer when I come back. I know there's an audience for my work. I know there are people out there who want to publish my books and buy my books. That's really very comforting. On the other hand, it's harder because I want to take risks. God knows I don't want to write the same novel over and over again, because it's boring. I have to keep myself interested, engaged for the two or three years the writing takes. Also, I try to attempt something different with each book, or at least I demand more of myself in terms of the craft.

Is your original conception of a novel anything like the finished product?
SI: When the work is in your mind, it doesn't exist. It hasn't truly been created. It has the element of not only fiction, but also of fantasy. I can imagine that a story will be a beautiful whole. It will fall together in the most felicitous fashion, and everyone will stop what they're doing, start reading, and gasp with pleasure. Before a book is written, you can savor all sorts of silly, grandiose fantasies—like being on David Letterman or receiving the Pulitzer Prize. The reality is usually somewhat less thrilling.

Like with life?
SI: Like with life. How many things are as good or better than our imagination makes them out to be?

Do you enjoy touring, or do you prefer being the solitary writer? Do you long to get back to your work when you're on the road?
SI: When I'm writing, I just want to get it over with, except at the very end. Toward the end of the novel, it comes together as well as it's going to, and I have the voice—and I have my people. I have created a world. You know, there's a reason why we earn our livings telling ourselves stories behind closed doors. If we didn't need the isolation, we would probably be writing screenplays or advertising copy. I find living in a universe I have fashioned very satisfying. Reality can be okay. But when I get out on a book tour, it's not like getting back into the real world and having lunch with a friend. A book tour is going from city to city delivering variations of a vaudeville routine six or seven times a day. You do meet some lovely and interesting people, but you're doing your job: being *The Novelist.* Although that character may be very close to who you are, you're still an actor in character. And then you're off to the next city.

When you aspired to be a writer, did you realize you were also going to be a performer?

SI: No. There are some people who really enjoy it. There's a whole world of academic novelists who go around the circuit reading. If a writer's work isn't selling enormously well, at least these readings give the writer a certain ego gratification and a chance to promote his or her work. Most writers, however, no longer write to be read aloud. They write to be read. And for those of us who do write to be read, I'm curious what's going to happen: Are we going to have one particular section of the book that's written as a performance piece? Where does the novel end and the drama begin?

When you write, are you aware that you may someday be reading your book aloud?

SI: In most cases, I just read my first chapter. With a mystery, there's not much else you can do without a tedious explication of the plot.

As a writer, you not only have to be a performer, but a business person as well. Was this difficult for you?

SI: I have fewer problems now. As with any business, you have to become smart for your own protection. Again, women have a more difficult time because we're not brought up to read the business pages, and we're not brought up to be responsible for doing our income taxes—or saying no to anyone or anything. We've been raised to be congenial. We have to learn to be strong.

Do you feel any responsibility to convey these ideas through your female characters; to make them strong and self-reliant?

SI: No. To tell you the truth, I subscribe to a quote that's usually attributed to Samuel Goldwyn: "If you want to send a message, call Western Union." Of course feminism figures in my writing. I am a contemporary woman: I have lived through a great social revolution, which has changed my life and my thinking. I can't *not* write about it. But I'm a realistic novelist, not a propagandist.

Do you ever struggle not to make your characters nice and polite? Is it difficult to show other sides of the female personality?

SI: No. I don't struggle. To the contrary. It's easier to create a whole, flawed human being than someone with a perpetual smile and no underarm stubble. Even though my characters may be lower-middle class, and even though they may be victims to a greater or lesser extent, they're women who have strengths and, occasionally, great courage. I have very little desire to write about wimps. This is not to say I make my female characters superhuman. But there are so many characters who are passive, or passive-aggressive in the Emma Bovary, Anna Karenina mold rather than strong women like Moll Flanders or Jane Eyre. Jane Eyre was heroic. I'll tell you where you find strong women these days. You find strong women in mysteries; especially in the private investigators. You find strong women in mysteries and in some of the work of women of color. White women in mainstream fiction are a great disappointment to me. Even in the nineties they don't seem to be able to transcend their own genitalia. They react only as wives, or as mothers, or as friends of other women, or as lovers. All their interests have to do with some facet of being women. Except for the rare novel, women characters seem unable to get past all the old stuff and think of issues that have nothing to do with them being women: War, poverty, social class, race, religion—anything. The world has opened up a great deal in the past twenty-five or thirty years. Where have the novelists been? You'd think some of them would have gotten out of the house or would have been touched by issues that go beyond guys—or children. I'm very interested in why they have not.

What about the women you encounter on your tour. Are you pleased by the type of women who read your books?

SI: Yes. I'm pleased and surprised. Some of the women are my age, some of them are non-women—a.k.a. men. Some of the women are quite a bit older or quite a bit younger than I. I've met women in their twenties, and some of them say, "My mother told me to read this, and I figured, how good could it be if she recommended it? But it was." That's fun.

What advice do you give young writers? What's the most important thing you can tell them?

SI: I tell them the normal things. I tell them to *write*. It's a job. Go to work. My other advice is to avoid writing courses. I say that because as a new writer you're terribly, terribly tender. Writers are always vulnerable, but even more so at the beginning. You wind up hearing criticism about adverbial clauses and character development; criticism that has very little to do with writing, because a good writer may not work on those things until the second or third draft. But this type of criticism can assume huge proportions because you're so fragile. You can not only lose sight of what you're doing, you can feel you're not equal to the task. That's number one. Number two, and this is even worse, in writing classes you start writing for someone else. You write to please someone, and it's usually the person teaching the course. When you do that, you lose the sound of your own voice—and that's all you have as a writer. Of course some fine writers, such as Mary Gordon, can go into a writing class and survive. But Gordon has a strong voice, and, I bet, a strong sense of self. Most new writers don't. Writing classes produce a lot of lifeless, short fiction written in the present tense. Does this work do anyone any good? I don't think so. You get a lot of imitation Raymond Carver or Anne Tyler. Raymond Carver did Raymond Carver beautifully. Anne Tyler is a great Anne Tyler; we don't need another one. In writing classes, students writing what they think someone else wants, or what is "right" lose their ability to be Mary Smith or Joe Shmo and tell the story that's unique to them. It's a terrible, terrible danger.

KATHERINE VAZ

*K*ATHERINE VAZ is a first-time novelist. Her book *Saudade* explores various aspects of her Portuguese heritage and notions about language and the senses. She is a graduate of the Programs in Writing at the University of California at Irvine, where she received her master of fine arts degree. Vaz is also a 1993 recipient of a Grant Fellowship from the National Endowment for the Arts. More than a dozen of her short stories have appeared in literary magazines and quarterlies; two were nominated for Pushcart Prizes, and one was cited in *The Best American Short Stories 1990* as one of the top one hundred stories of 1989. Vaz is currently working on a collection of short stories and a second novel.

Why do you write?
KV: When I was twelve years old, I was sitting in a classroom doing a writing assignment. We had to use the vocabulary word of the day or some simple exercise like that. I remember this feeling coming over me, and although I didn't know where the feeling was coming from, I knew I wanted to have it for the rest of my life. That was really the moment when I decided what I was going to do. I wish I could remember what I'd written, but I don't. I just remember the sensation of a power coming over me. I need to write. That's really the answer to "why I write." There's nothing else I could imagine doing with my life.

What did you do about this feeling?
KV: I didn't tell anyone. I think I was confused by it at first. I wrote stories and poems from about the time I was twelve, and I never quit. I didn't really know how it was going to all add up. I didn't have a well-thought-out plan. I didn't think, "Gee, I'll do this and this and this, and then I'll be a writer."

Where are you from originally?
KV: I grew up in the East Bay Area of San Francisco. I went to the University of California at Santa Barbara, and I spent my last year at the University of Sussex, England. I spent a small amount of time in upstate New York, and then I moved to San Francisco and then to Los Angeles. I jumped around a lot, and I often went back to Portugal to visit the Azores, where my father's family is from. About the time I started to develop my writer's voice, I realized the subjects of colors and language and the Azorean sensibility were what I wanted to write about. These areas seemed very suggestive to me.

Is your novel about Portugal?
SV: The novel is based on the Portuguese people, or Luso-Americans, in California, and how they find life and art in the world around them. About a quarter of the book takes place in the Azores, and the rest takes place in California. The title of my novel is *Saudade.* This is a Portuguese word which is difficult to translate. One definition is that *Saudade* means a kind of intense longing for what is absent from one's life, until that becomes the greatest presence. It's a beautiful word. I define it on the title page. I tried to pick another title that was more recognizable, but that was the one I kept coming back to.

How did you get to the writers program?
KV: I took a long route. My first job after college was as an editor at a magazine. Because the turnover rate at the magazine was so

high, I made contacts with people at many of the major newspapers and magazines in the California area. As a result, I was able to make a living as a freelance writer after I left my job. I was a freelance writer for about eight years. I also wrote a couple of nonfiction books—a swimming book as well as several diet and exercise books, which helped finance my fiction writing. I knew I was a writer when I was twelve, but I really began to concentrate on writing fiction when I was about seventeen. I would set my alarm and get up to work. I went to a school run by Spanish nuns, so they instilled a sense of discipline in me. To this day, I get up every morning by six o'clock, and then I work until noon. Even when I was younger, I would sit there, whether or not something came to me. I see now that this was a lot of the groundwork in terms of teaching myself to write. I was writing a lot of short stories at this time, and I had a number of them accepted by various literary magazines. I also had friends who were very helpful. One heard about the writing program at Irvine and suggested I try it because I was getting tired of freelance work. I thought I'd like to be in a program where I had lots of time and support. That's what the program at Irvine offered. Everyone in the program receives a fellowship. I like the fact that they only accept six people every year. There is a lot of personal attention. But more than that, the program gave me a lot of time. At one point I realized I was no longer writing short stories. I was writing something that felt like a novel. I didn't sit down with a well-sketched-out idea when I started. Although I went to the workshops, and I participated in the program, the teachers' attitude was always, "Just keep doing what you're doing. You seem to be on some sort of path. We'll leave you alone." I had been working as a writer for a while, and I knew that now was my chance to have the time to do some good work. I really used my time. I practically locked myself in for three years. Although I had friends I had met through the program, I didn't go out that much. I just stayed in and worked.

How did you put your novel together?

KV: I would not necessarily recommend the method I used for writing my first novel, except that it worked for me. I had masses and masses of stuff, and I didn't know how to fit it together. I didn't have what we call the "arc" or the overall form. I had a massive number of pages, lots of what I thought of as tinsel on the tree, and I couldn't see the tree anymore. I wanted to load everything on, which is a first-time novelist's mistake. I cringe when I think of it now, because I realized that part of what art is, is knowing how to create the design. I remember looking at my pages and sighing. I thought I was done. I had spent three years of solid work on it, but in actuality, I had this stack of scenes, and I knew that now I had to start writing the book. By that point I was putting in between twelve and sixteen hours a day, seven days a week. I was coming to the finish line. I spent the entire summer rewriting my book before I could sell it. It was exhausting. For a month after I finished, I couldn't even read magazines. I was stretched thin.

What were the benefits of the writers program?

KV: The writer's program put me in touch with people who were doing what I was doing. It also gave me the time and the atmosphere to write. My teachers, Oakley Hall and Mcdonald Harris, were very supportive. I also received a grant to travel back to the Azores and do a little bit more research. The program helped in that way. I was in a room but I didn't feel lonely. I didn't feel isolated from the world. There were other writers around, and that type of "spiritual community" helped me.

Were there any drawbacks to the program?

KV: So much depends on the people who are in the workshops with you. That can really make a difference. I do think writers need readers and people who can act as editors, but I don't think writing by committee is a good idea.

Is that dangerous? Can a young writer risk losing her voice through this type of "committee" feedback?

KV: A young writer can definitely lose the voice that he or she is working on. The people making the suggestions tend to be very intelligent, but not everyone is a good editor. I think every writer needs editors who see the rules and the world that he or she is trying to create on the page, and they can hold the writer to those rules. A good editor allows a writer's voice to find its own way. A writer has to have a very strong personality. You have to know who you are and what you're trying to do. At the same time, however, you can't be so arrogant that you shut yourself off and never listen when a good editor or reader tells you the truth. You need well-read people who have your best interests in mind. The larger committee can sand down the edges of things in a way that's unfortunate, and I hate to see that happen. You must stick to what you believe in, especially when you're working on a novel. You're the only one who can teach yourself how to write the novel. The novel tells you what to do. It instructs you about how it is going to be written. That's the voice you have to listen to.

How would you define the process of writing?

KV: There are two attitudes about the process of writing. One is that you control what goes down. You sketch it out and it follows your rules. It's a world you create. It's the god-like stance toward writing. But then there's the attitude that you are more subservient. You are the one getting the orders. I prefer that attitude, because I like the sensation of suddenly writing something and not quite knowing where this or that turn came from. It's as if it rode in on a shaft of light. Sometimes a character will suddenly seem more alive than I had planned on. That's the writing telling me what to do. When you allow this to happen, more surprising things can come out. I think it's a mistake to say, "Oh, I have a good idea," and then march characters and language through a course like a maze. They might rebel. It's the same as going out with friends and saying, "Okay, I'm going to say this, and the other person will say that, and we'll do this, and this is how it's going to turn out." That never happens. You start with a rough idea, and then you go out and see what happens. I like that attitude toward writing much better. You need to be a good listener.

How long is the writer's program?
KV: Two years.

Did you finish your novel about the time the program was over?
KV: No. There again, I was lucky. My novel took a little over three years, but I was able to get teaching assignments for that extra year. You have to keep in mind that the work will take the time it takes. Just when you think it's finished, it will resist for some odd reason. A writer has to be patient with the work and let it get finished when it's ready.

Patience is very hard for writers. You don't just have to have patience for the writing, you have to wait to hear from agents and from publishers.
KV: I think you should send out your work and then forget about it. It's very hard to do, but the business side of writing uses a whole different side of your brain, and it requires a different kind of patience. The waiting always takes longer than one thinks. I knew this from my nonfiction writing. I remember waiting for contracts, and especially waiting for the checks. Sometimes it takes months. A young writer who's going into a

writing program and says, "I'll finish my book in two years, and then within a month or so I'll have a check," is wrong. It just doesn't happen that way. I had a friend who gave me some very good advice. She said, "You should allow only fifteen minutes a day to think about the business side of writing. After that, put it out of your head." Try and put those things aside, because they can make you crazy. And they really don't have much to do with the job of writing.

How did you get an agent?

KV: Another benefit of the writer's program is that you meet writers who have agents. If they like your work, they will recommend you. A friend in the program had an agent in New York, and she mentioned me to this woman. She mentioned my name a year before I was even finished with my book. When the time came, the agent read my book twice. The only thing she suggested, aside from some minor corrections, was that I rewrite the beginning. Then she sent it out. Part of the function of an agent is being a kind of matchmaker. She picked an editor who had published books that were very similar to the style in which I had written mine. It was the first person she showed it to, and the publishing house where the editor worked agreed to buy it. The whole process took approximately ten or twelve weeks between the time of sending it out to an agent and getting it accepted by an editor. That's actually a very fast response.

How did you feel when you got the call from your agent?

KV: I was so happy to have finished my book that in a way I forgot the part about selling it. I was so happy to have just hit that point.

What are you working on now?

KV: I'm currently working on two books at once. One is a collection of short stories, and the other is my next novel. I can't quite predict how long either one of them is going to take. I'm a slow writer. I write out everything first by hand. Then I put it on the computer, and then I print it out. I make all my corrections with a pencil on the printout, and then I type in my corrections. That is the kind of busy work I'll do at night if I'm tired. I print it out again, and go over it again as many times as I need before it's finished.

Why did you choose to write novels rather than screenplays?
KV: That's the form my words take when I begin to put them on a page. I guess I think and feel in novels.

You're right on the brink of having your book Saudade published. How do you think your life is going to change?
KV: I hope there's something about my work that moves people, and I want to contribute something of what I am. Beyond that, I think it's important for writers to protect their solitude as much as possible and go on to the next book. It's very dangerous to get caught up in external things like reviews and promotions. I have a peaceful rhythm in my life that helps me work, and I hope that doesn't change. I swim a lot in the pool that's nearby, and I plan on getting married next year.

Is he a writer?
KV: No. Michael is, however, a very big reader, and he's very smart about living with a writer. It can be very difficult for the person you live with, when you're wandering around the house and not saying anything. It's not because you're mad, but because there are voices in your head and phrases you might use, floating in and out.

Do you have any particular advice for aspiring writers?
KV: There's really a very limited amount of advice to give. The individual writer will discover almost everything on his or her own. I can say this: From the moment you decide that you are a

writer, don't wait for the time you think you should begin. *That* is the moment you should begin. The biggest mistake is that although people have a dream of being a writer, they don't do it because they think they're not ready, or they think that when they're twenty-five or so they'll have enough time or money or experience, and they can begin. That moment never comes. One should simply start the process.

What pressures and expectations are there in moving on to a second novel?

KV: There are pressures in two ways. If a writer's first book does well, there's the pressure to equal it. If the first one doesn't do well, then there's the question of what's going to happen with the second one. It's better to ignore all of that, actually. It puts static into your head and drowns out what you're trying to listen to. Writers need to love their work, not in a blind or silly or defensive way, but in a way that remembers what went into nurturing the book and knows what its weak points might be. That's hard. Watching on the sidelines as it goes out into the world is a bit like sending a child off to school and hoping he does well. You spend all those years telling the child how wonderful he is, and he goes off to school and gets beaten up. It breaks your heart, but you dust the child off and say, "I still think you're beautiful."

WENDY WASSERSTEIN

ENDY WASSERSTEIN was born in Brooklyn, New York, and is a graduate of Mount Holyoke College and the Yale Drama School. Her 1988 play *The Heidi Chronicles* won the Tony Award and the Pulitzer Prize. She is also the author of *Uncommon Women and Others* and *Isn't It Romantic?* Her 1993 play *The Sisters Rosensweig* won five Tony Awards. Wasserstein's screen credits include: *The Object of My Affection,* which was based on the book by Stephen McCauley. Her collection of essays is entitled *Bachelor Girls.* Wasserstein lives in New York City.

Why do you write?
WW: When I was growing up I remember thinking that my family was very funny. I remember watching sitcoms like "Make Room for Daddy," and thinking my family was funnier than they were, and that the people didn't seem like real people. I also grew up in New York, and I grew up going to the theater. I've always loved being inside a theater. I find it both exciting and calming, in some sense, the way you feel when you're home. I'm vaguely shy, so I wouldn't be much of an actor or director. The other level is that I've always been sort of funny, and I got on in life by being funny. I'm observant as well. So I can see how it all bolts from my affection for the theater and from my personality. I can see why it happened.

Did you write as a child? Did you keep a diary?
WW: I did keep a little diary when I was a kid, but I didn't write in it a lot. I remember thinking about shows. I remember playing with dolls and thinking what shows they would be in. They were mostly musicals. I didn't "write write" per se, but I remember thinking about it a lot.

I read that you had a difficult time deciding between business school and drama school. Do you remember anything about this process? Do you have any advice for young people about making these types of decisions?
WW: It was very hard to make this decision. It scared me. I knew that with business school, I could make a living. In some ways it would have been more of a regular life. I can see that. Actually my brother helped me, and oddly enough, he's in business. If there's something you really want to do in life and it's scary, you should still try and see what happens.

While **The Sisters Rosensweig** *is in some ways about identity, isn't it also about accepting who you are? Why do you think women are so hard on themselves?*
WW: I think everyone is hard on themselves—both men and women. All that stuff from the seventies—all of that "having it all"—was lethal. Who can do that? Women put pressure on themselves to do all these things. I remember when I spoke at Radcliffe a few years ago. The students were saying, "How could you not know what you wanted to do when you were a sophomore?" I kept thinking, "Well, yes, but you need to take the time to find out what you want." There have always been these images of women. We were never thin enough, and now we're not successful,

or sexy enough either. It's never adequate. For some reason we're always being judged, and of course, the worse judge is ourself.

Do you think attitudes have changed since you wrote **The Heidi Chronicles?** *Are young women as hard on themselves now?*
WW: Young women are very hard on themselves. The difference between these women and my generation is that we came at the beginning of the shift. The idea of "having it all" was just coming in, in the sense that sometimes it seemed you had to choose between a career and a personal life. Because the opportunities weren't there for women, sometimes on a scale of one to ten, you had to give your career a ten. By concentrating so much on career, sometimes the personal issues were neglected. I don't think that's as true for younger women because the opportunities are more open. Law schools and medical schools now have about fifty percent women. If you read about Supreme Court Justice Ruth Bader Ginsburg and her life as a young lawyer, you find that the opportunities just weren't there, despite her education and intelligence.

And now they are?
WW: And now they are on some levels. I think that's gotten slightly better.

Are you disciplined with your writing?
WW: No. I'm terrible. I always mean to get up in the morning and exercise, write, and have a lovely conversation with a friend. I'm terribly *un*disciplined. I'm not good at organization. I should be writing, but I'm on the phone instead. When I know something is due, I'll actual-

ly sit down and write. In my head, I've decided to start a new play in January. I know that in January I'm going to write. I'll take myself to the library and work every day.

Is that where you write?
WW: Yes. I don't work at home. I work at the library, or I work in an office. I can't work at home.

Does that come from studying in school?
WW: No. It comes from the fact that when I'm writing, I'm happy to be interrupted. I've always loved libraries. In elementary school, I used to go to the King's Highway Library in Brooklyn. In the library, everyone else is working, so I start working too.

Do you find you're more productive when you're content or when you're melancholy?
WW: No. I'm more productive when I'm in a disciplined mode. When I set the time aside to write, nothing will keep me from working.

Do you solve any of your writing problems in dreams?
WW: No, but I'll think about a play for a long time before I write it. Sometimes something will click in, and I'll think about it. It's not really dreaming; it's more like daydreaming.

Do you keep notes when you're daydreaming?
WW: No, not a lot. Sometimes I'll write down a little outline about the characters.

You said you're beginning a new play in January. Will it change a lot between daydreaming and actual writing?
WW: Yes. Different things will happen. In *The Sisters*

Rosensweig, I didn't know the sister Gorgeous would be that funny. It was really a play about Sara; a woman who had closed up. The play was about bringing love into her life again. Gorgeous was just a subsidiary character.

Did the play become funnier as you wrote it?
WW: Yes, and I had people like Madeline Kahn and Linda Lavin, who are such great comedians.

How does winning awards affect your writing?
WW: In some ways it's helpful. I'm one of those people who tends to be self-negating, so in a sense it's helpful because ultimately you have that award. In a way it does add pressure because you think, "Oh God, I can't dupli- cate this. Everyone's going to hate me now." You think all those wonderful thoughts. What's bad about it is being in a competitive mode. You think, "Oh, I have to win this." That's horrible. I hate awards for that, and because they hurt people. Robert Klein wasn't nominated for a Tony. I was quite saddened by that. He did such a wonderful job, and I thought, "Why hurt this man?" It doesn't take away from the excellence of what he did. So I don't like awards for that, but I do like the fact that they give you a sense of yourself; it's a sad thing, but they do somehow give you a sense of self that's yours.

Several of the women I've interviewed say they sometimes find it difficult not to be nice and polite in their writing. Do you ever struggle with this when you're developing characters?
WW: Yes. I'm very bad at being angry. I also try to please, and it's hard for me not to be funny.

Do you ever try and make your female characters mean or nasty?

WW: So many people make women mean and nasty, it's nice not to.

You talk about mothers and daughters in your plays. Why do we all have issues with our mothers? Has writing helped you resolve any of these issues?

WW: I don't know if writing has helped, but perhaps age has helped. My mother is a real character. We just had a birthday for my sister, and my mother sliced up a mango and put a candle in the middle of it. Of all the characters, this woman writes herself better than I ever could. The connection is so close between mothers and daughters, and their love is so deep; we also have a certain anger at them. It's a very close connection.

What advice do you give young playwrights?

WW: I tell them to keep writing and not undermine themselves. If you say, "This idea is terrible, I can't do it," then it won't get written. The most important thing is that you get your ideas on paper. What's great about play writing as opposed to movie or television writing, is that you can have people read the play out loud, and that's a wonderful thing. It's a great thing to put on plays. Ultimately, if you're putting on plays as a grownup on Broadway, in some ways it's no different than putting on plays in high school. You're putting on a show. It's a bunch of actors, a script, and a director. That's what is great about it. Even though the stakes are higher, you get to play for the rest of your life.

How bad can that be?

WW: That's right. How bad can that be? Of course, it can also be horrible and scary. You can get terrible reviews, and the play can not work. On the other hand, it can be great. If you become a stockbroker, or whatever, you won't get to play for the rest of your life. There's something swell about that.

MARGARET ATWOOD

ARGARET ATWOOD was born in Ottawa, Ontario. She is considered Canada's foremost contemporary writer, and she has published more than thirty-five books of fiction, poetry, and literary criticism. Atwood graduated from the University of Toronto, received a master's degree from Radcliffe College, and studied Victorian fantasy at Harvard University. She has won many prestigious awards and has received several honorary degrees. Her novels include: *The Edible Woman, Lady Oracle, Life Before Man, Bodily Harm, The Handmaid's Tale, Cat's Eye, Good Bones,* and *The Robber Bride.* Her collections of short stories include *Dancing Girls* and *Wilderness Tips.* Her novel *The Handmaid's Tale* was adapted for the screen by Harold Pinter. Atwood's books have been published in more than twenty-five countries and have been translated into more than twenty languages. She lives in Toronto with novelist Graeme Gibson and their daughter.

Why do you write?
MA: I write because I'm a writer. It's what I do. That may seem very simple, but every culture has always had storytellers and artists. It seems to be part of being human for a society to possess artists.

In this era of visual images, do you think the written word still has the same power?
MA: The same power as what? For most of history, the majority of

the population has not been able to read. That doesn't mean the word has had no power, because literature was oral. It's true that we now live in an age of visual images. We also live in an age of "musical images," but we still live in a society in which language is the way we communicate most of the time. So compared with, say, the fifteenth century, we're much more literate; that is, a larger percentage of the population reads. If you look at the number of books that are published every year, it's really quite astonishing.

At what age did you realize you wanted to be a writer?
MA: Sixteen.

What form did your words take?
MA: I wrote pretty bad poems. I also wrote prose fiction and prose nonfiction, just as I do now.

Did you think your poems were bad at the time?
MA: No. I loved them. I thought they were wonderful.

Did you keep a journal?
MA: I've never been very good at keeping journals. It's too regular an activity for me.

Do you keep little notes?
MA: I make a lot of notes. I certainly keep a notebook and a lot of scraps of paper. I'll write on anything. I write on menus if I don't have anything else handy.

What do you do with these little notes?
MA: I keep them, and sooner or later they come in handy. When I'm writing a novel, I accumulate quite a pile of them, and I carry them around in a file folder.

Are you generally very organized?
MA: I feel quite disorganized, but I realize that in order to do what I do, I must actually be fairly organized.

How has the situation for women writers changed since you began writing? Are there as many obstacles to overcome?

MA: I think there are possibly fewer obstacles. It's not quite such a freaky thing to be. It's not quite such a freaky thing to be a successful woman in any field. I think women still have a certain guilty feeling that they shouldn't be successful, or that they shouldn't display power. Women, especially in the early stages of their careers, have to fight against this feeling. They have to fight against the feeling that they should just be "nice." In order to be a writer with any power, some of what you say is not going to be nice. In order to express the full range of human feelings, you have to go against the image of women as always being kind, polite, and nurturing.

How does a young woman develop that? Do you think either you have it or you don't?

MA: I think you either have the motivation or you don't. Writing is either something you want to do, or it's something you don't want to do. If you don't want to do it, then presumably it's not a problem. If you do want to do it, then it has to be something you want to *do* rather than something you want to *be*. You have to know the difference. Some people would like to just wake up famous without doing the work.

Do you think people choose the profession because of the image and the possibility of fame?

MA: Some do—or else they choose it because they think it's easy. They think anybody can do it. But in fact, writing is a gambler's area because there are no guarantees and no pension plans. There's nothing that says just because you work hard, you're going to be successful. You have to be very motivated and stick with it.

Do you think young people today tend to glamorize the image of a writer?

MA: They're more likely to glamorize being a rock singer or being a movie star. But a lot of young people who have gotten past the first level are quite committed to their writing. It's what they want to do.

What is the question you get asked most often by young writers?

MA: "How do I get published?"

What do you tell them?

MA: It's certainly a pertinent question. But again there are no rules, and there is no formula. What many young writers do—and it is certainly what I did—is to send their work to small magazines.

Is that how you started?

MA: Absolutely. And if that doesn't work, you can always start your own small magazine.

I interviewed a poet in San Francisco who said it only takes one piece of paper to start a newsletter.

MA: That's right. Now that we have computers, you can do these things a lot more easily than you could when I was starting. There are many ways of beginning and many ways of communicating.

What traits does a writer need?

MA: Writing is like walking over Niagara Falls blindfolded. You have to convince yourself that all you need to do is keep putting one foot in front of the other, and that there's no waterfall. It's like saying, "I'm not going to think about what the odds are, because if I do, I'll be too scared."

The odds never change with any creative profession. Once you publish a book, there's no guarantee you will ever publish anything else.

MA: No. That's right. Nor does it mean that if you do publish another book, it will be well received.

So you're always walking over Niagra Falls?
MA: You're always starting. With every book, you're always starting on page one.

Have you ever considered stopping?
MA: If I get to the point where I'm not interested in what I'm doing, or if I thought I was just repeating myself, I would stop. Part of it is that I like trying new things, and of course writing is learning as well. You learn something every time you write. I suppose I'm a curious person.

What kinds of things do you learn?
MA: That varies from book to book. You certainly learn different things about writing itself. You try things you've never done before, difficult things. You stretch yourself, and then, of course, you learn the subject matter of your book. In my latest book, for instance, one of my characters is a female military historian, so I had to learn something about that.

Do you also learn about yourself, and is that ever painful?
MA: A lot of people say writing is painful, and sometimes it is painful. Unless there were a positive counterbalance, however, I don't think anyone would do it. In other words, there are enormous rewards as well.

Do you think writing is a form of self-analysis?
MA: It can be that, or it can be an analysis of the world, or both. There isn't just one type of writing. There are many different kinds, and every writer is an individual. It's a very personal thing.

What similarities are there between the language of poetry and the language of the novel?

MA: If you're a conscientious and devoted writer, you want to use language well in both prose and poetry. The difference is the wavelength of the novel. It's much longer. In other words, if you're dealing with 550 pages, the connections between the parts of that work are going to be a different shape than if you're dealing with one page. One page is very condensed. Think of it as a graph, for example, the kind of graph that shows your heartbeat. Just stretch the graph out and that's a novel. If you condense it, that's a poem.

Do you have any preference for writing poetry or prose, or do you just write them at different times in your life?
MA: I write them at different times in my life.

When you're seized by different passions?
MA: By different wavelengths.

Please describe the room where you write.
MA: I write in my study, which is on the second floor of my house. There are three desks in the room. One is a little oak roll-top desk where I keep my notepaper for writing personal letters. One is a kind of table with drawers underneath where I keep my work in progress, and the third desk is where I actually work. It has my computer, all my pens and pencils, my erasers, and all of those kinds of things. The tools.

What do you see out the window?
MA: I try not to look out the window. It's too distracting. If I did look out the window, I'd see my front garden where I spend a lot of time.

Do you have anything on the walls of your study?
MA: I have a print above my third desk, by an artist named David Blackwood. The second desk faces the window. The first desk has

one of those oak dividers with little compartments that's probably from an old mail room. There is a winged toad above it.

Do you pick these things deliberately?
MA: Yes, I pick them deliberately. They're fitting for what I'm writing at the moment. I change them from time to time. On the other walls I have bookshelves; above one bookshelf I have a drawing by my daughter, one by myself, a book-jacket design— that sort of thing.

Do you let other people into your space, or is it very private?
MA: They walk in whether I let them in or not. If you have a family, people walk in on you all the time. I have one of those "Do not disturb" signs, which nobody pays attention to.

Is there any particular advice you give writers?
MA: Read and write. It's the only advice.

Are there any particular books you recommend?
MA: You can't tell people what to read, because they will discover that for themselves.

I know this may sound obvious, but why is reading so valuable?
MA: Reading is valuable for a writer in the same way that listening to music is valuable for a musician. It's how you learn your language of communication.

Can reading all this great stuff be intimidating to a young writer?
MA: You don't have to read great stuff.

People should read lousy stuff?
MA: You will find what you need to read. The things that are of no interest to you won't register, and the things that are of interest will. And if you're going to be intimidated, then you're not going to be a writer anyway.

BEBE MOORE CAMPBELL

*B*EBE MOORE CAMPBELL is the author of *Sweet Summer: Growing Up With and Without My Dad, Successful Women/Angry Men, Your Blues Ain't Like Mine,* and *Sisters and Brothers.* She has been a winner of the National Endowment for the Arts Literature Grant, the National Association of Negro Business and Professional Women's Literature Award, and the Midwestern Radio Theater Workshop Competition. She is a contributing editor of *Essence* magazine, and her work has appeared in *Black Enterprise, Savvy, MS., Ebony,* the *New York Times Magazine,* the *Washington Post,* and the *Los Angeles Times.* Bebe Moore Campbell was born in Philadelphia and received a B.S. degree in elementary education from the University of Pittsburgh. She lives in Los Angeles with her husband, daughter, and stepson.

Why do you write?
BMC: I write to heal. I feel very responsible as a member of the African-American community. I'm aware of the pain and the anger, as well as the joy. I hope my writing not only heals the anger of that community but of the larger community of Americans as well. I want to spread understanding, and through my characters I want to offer alternatives for human behavior. If I can show why my characters are the way they

are, and let them act out some of the turmoil and some of the issues that face blacks, whites, Asians, and Latinos, the characters can become a reference to teach the reader.

Did the violence in Los Angeles and the current climate of fear affect your writing?
BMC: Oh, yes. Everything is much more intense now and much more at risk. We're living in a more volatile, mixed-up community. I feel the need for healing. People need a way to expunge their pain and their rage.

Have you always felt a responsibility as a writer?
BMC: Yes, and I know where this responsibility comes from. When I was growing up, my mother presented me with books by authors such as Harriet Tubman and Sojourner Truth. These women became my heroes. I grew up wanting to be like them. I always wanted to "save the race." While I knew I couldn't do that, I did want to make a contribution.

Did you always want to become a writer?
BMC: I always liked writing. I didn't realize I wanted to be a writer until after high school or maybe even college. I was in a creative writing class in the third grade, but I didn't have a sense that I wanted to be published until after I graduated from college. I wrote poetry and short stories when I was younger.

What changed for you after college?
BMC: I don't know. The desire to express myself in print just intensified. Once I got away from the constraints of college and I had more time, I wrote more. Gradually writing became what I did every day.

Did growing up in the sixties affect your desire to write?

BMC: Yes. There was a coming of age in the sixties. Although there were all these intense feelings about civil rights and about what was happening in the streets of America, there was no place to put them. For me, the place to put my feelings was on the page.

Describe your writing environment.
BMC: It's a terrible looking office. It's going to be fixed up this year. It's my own private space, but it is truly horrible.

Why is it horrible?
BMC: Because we fixed up the other part of the house first. My room is downstairs in the basement. It has a really ratty bathroom. It's an L-shaped room. The house was built around 1929, and I think my room was probably the housekeeper's room.

Do you have things pasted on the walls?
BMC: I have one wall full of pictures of my heroes—my *she*roes. I have pictures of Dorothy Dandridge, Sojourner Truth, Harriet Tubman, Lorraine Hansberry, Ida B. Wells Barnett, and people like that. I have another wall of awards I've received. There's a table with a computer, plus a file cabinet, and a desk.

Do *you write on the typewriter, word processor, or on yellow pads in longhand?*
BMC: I compose on the computer. I'm not computer literate. I use the computer as a kind of glorified typewriter.

What kind of schedule do you keep?
BMC: (Laughter)

Do you keep a schedule?
BMC: When I finish talking with you, I'll go down and work

on my book because I didn't write today. I had to work on an
Essence article. This is the last magazine article I will write
until I finish my book.

What time do you start writing in the morning?

BMC: I get up at nine. I'm a late riser. Every writer I know is a
sensible morning person who gets up around five o'clock and
works. That makes so much sense. I'm a night owl, however,
and I don't go to bed until one or two o'clock in the morning. I get up at nine and I fool around and waste a lot of time.
I don't get started working until around ten or eleven, and
then I have to stop at three to get my daughter at school. I
come home and make dinner and then manage to snatch a
few hours of work. It would be very simple if I could get up by
seven o'clock. Somehow it all gets done. Although I have better days than others, I really don't want to write more than
four hours a day.

Why?

BMC: I think that's enough! To sit down at a computer and
write for four or five hours and still have time for other
things. That's the life I envision for myself.

Why do you think discipline is so hard for writing?

BMC: I don't know. I love to write. I love to sit down and do
it. Ultimately, I do have a routine. In the last six weeks, I've
written a chapter and a seventy-five-page outline. In my
career, I've written three other books, so obviously I have a
routine. I know it sounds haphazard, but the more I get into
it, the better my writing becomes, and I develop a more rigid
schedule. The beginning, or writing the first draft, is the
hardest part. I love to revise, and I love to rewrite.

What is the name of the new novel?

BMC: *Brothers and Sisters.* It's fiction. The book looks at black–white and male–female relationships in Los Angeles in the aftermath of April 29th.*

Do you find it difficult to switch from nonfiction to fiction?

BMC: No. I really started with fiction and then went to nonfiction. In the beginning, I wrote stories, and although I wanted to write novels, I got sidetracked and was pulled into doing magazine work. I wrote articles to support myself. Sometimes I wonder if there was a quality I had with my early fiction that I don't have any more. It may not have been good writing. I don't know what it was, but there was a different kind of energy that has been replaced. I'm certain I'm better at the craft, but there's something I used to have before I got into magazine work that I don't have now.

Is it something you want back?

BMC: I can't even remember what it was, but I think it was a different kind of energy. It may have been just youthful writing, and it may not have been very good. After all, those were the stories people turned down.

Ideally, would you prefer to write only fiction?

BMC: Yes. I enjoy writing for magazines, but I don't enjoy sandwiching it in with writing books. That's just craziness. It breaks my flow and my concentration. It makes me evil.

What have you learned about yourself as a writer? What strengths or weaknesses have you discovered?

BMC: I've learned that no matter what, I will do my work. Sometimes to my detriment, I wish I could let go. I'm very

---

*On April 29, 1992, riots erupted in Los Angeles following a not-guilty verdict in the trial of four police officers accused of beating Rodney King.

much work driven. I can see this in my family, particularly with my father and with my father's brothers. My aunts were probably like this as well, except they didn't have a way to express it. There are deep strains of workaholism in my family. I'm talking about men with not much education who came out of rural North Carolina. In most cases, they didn't even have a high school degree, and yet they went out into the wide, wide world, and by golly, they made something of themselves. They owned stores and ran unions. My Uncle Eddy worked seven days a week in his grocery store. The images I have are of hard work.

What else have you learned?
BMC: I've also learned that I can write a novel. Everything I dreamed about doing, I found I can do. I learned that I like getting into my characters' heads and pretending to be each one of them. I enjoy coming from a lot of different points of view, and I also enjoy writing about both sexes.

Is it hard to probe into painful areas? For example, in **Sweet Summer: Growing Up With and Without My Dad,** *you wrote about your father who had died. What do you learn by pushing beyond areas that are "safe"?*
BMC: I guess there was some fear attached to writing that book. I think I've always written in fear of some sort. With my new book, there's a little less fear because I'm more sure of what I'm doing, or I think I am. What I wanted to do in *Sweet Summer,* was to tell as much truth as I could. Since I didn't want to hurt anyone, living or dead, there was always a balancing act, and that sort of stressed me out.

Were you a different person in any way when you started the book and when you finished it? Where had you arrived when you finished?
BMC: I had done my best, and I had said everything I wanted

to say. If there hadn't been the fear of offending someone, I might have gone deeper. But I'm not here to tell all my business. I told the story I wanted to tell. I told the story I felt safe telling. I guess I didn't push as much, and yet I did push. There were things I wrote and then thought, "Oh no, what's he going to say when he reads this?" There were some things I knew right on I wasn't going to say, things I wasn't going to reveal.

Is it easier to probe into these areas in nonfiction than in fiction?
BMC: It's easier with fiction, because the characters are not you.

Many people feel that part of being a writer is being able to take journeys that other people fear. Would you do it again? Would you write another autobiography?
BMC: Yes, somewhere down the line, I believe I will. People often ask, "What happened to Michael?" He's my cousin, and I wrote about him in *Sweet Summer.*

What lessons or what wisdom do you hope your daughter will gain by reading books by African-American women and by women in genral?
BMC: My daughter is artistically talented. She sings, she acts, and she writes. I think these books will give her permission to do all the things I was given permission to do so many years ago when my mother handed me a book and said it had been written by her sorority sister. She meant that it had been written by a black woman. I read everything I could get my hands on, and yet I hadn't read anything by a black person, let alone a black woman. This was a different feeling that said to me, "You too can write a book." I hope my daughter can read all these wonderful things and be challenged to go even higher with her creations.

Do you encourage young people to read?
BMC: Yes. I visit a lot of schools. I spoke to about 1,000 kids at

a junior high school recently. In the last novel I wrote, there was a young character the kids could identify with. I try and pull them in. When I go to the schools, I tell the students to read. This echoes in my own home because I read to my teenage daughter. I made a commitment that I wouldn't cut off bedtime stories at the age of eight.

Does success make writing any easier?
BMC: Money makes it easier. For so many years I wrote, and I struggled financially. I was never down and out because I always had an income, but there were times when I had to get loans from home. An article that I thought was going to be instantly accepted and bring me a check in the mail, would suddenly require a rewrite. That would throw everything out of balance. I lived through those times. And now, although I'm by no means getting the advances of Jackie Collins, I am making decent money. That makes the struggle easier, because now I can get my office fixed up. I think I'll write better in a nicer environment. I don't have worries like, "How am I going to pay my daughter's tuition?" I'm glad my success is coming now. After my father died, I had some money but I was really too young and too stupid to know how to spend it properly. I didn't just throw it in the street. I did some wise things, but now I really am much, much wiser. Writing also becomes easier with acceptance. Acceptance gives me confidence because it makes me feel my audience is growing.

What have you learned about publishing?
BMC: Publishing is a business. While I'm not a businessperson, I know that the bottom line is: If a publisher gives you X amount of money, they're going to promote you. They're not going to let your work die, because they've made an investment.

Do you have any advice about achieving goals?
BMC: Yes. Have goals. Set goals. Have a things-to-do book. Have a year's plan. Every year on New Year's day, set five things that you want to have happen that year. Associate with people who are about something; people who are about achieving. Associate with people who are like-minded, otherwise you are going to be with people who will ultimately try and pull you down. They may be envious that you have dreams, goals, and plans, and they don't. Watch who you go with romantically. Make sure your romantic partner has a goal, shares your vision, and supports your dream.

DENISE CHÁVEZ

*D*ENISE CHÁVEZ is a native of New Mexico. The title story from her book *The Last of the Menu Girls* won the Puerto del Sol fiction award for 1985. She has also written numerous plays that have been produced throughout the United States and in Europe. Chávez holds a master's degree in creative writing from the University of New Mexico and a master's degree in fine arts from Trinity University in San Antonio, Texas. Her most recent book of fiction is *Face of an Angel.* Denise Chávez writes in the room where she was born.

Why do you write?
DC: I want to communicate in ways I never thought I could when I was young. I started writing in my diary when I was eight years old. I don't think I had a lot of communication with people when I was young. I don't remember talking with my mother or with my sister very often. Writing was a way of being honest with people I couldn't be totally honest with face to face. My parents were divorced when I was about ten. That was very painful, and we didn't talk about it very much. Writing was always a confrontation, a way to deeply explore my feelings. I teach my writing classes that there are main rules in writing. One is to be honest. And one must never deliberately hurt people. For me, writing is a way of becoming an honest person.

*When you were writing in your diary, were you aware that some-
day you might want to become a writer?*

DC: Absolutely not. It never occurred to me "to be" a writer.
When I was in the second grade or so, it began to dawn on
me that I enjoyed writing. Somewhere in one of my boxes, I
have what I consider to be my first short story. It was about a
tree. When I wrote it, I thought "Gee, that's really neat." It
felt really good to write. I was able to express some heartfelt
feelings. When I was in high school, I'd put articles I liked in
my diaries. These later became notebooks, and eventually I
started writing some of my own poetry and short stories. I
never thought there was anything in it, until I was a senior in
college. I won fifteen dollars in a literary contest for the best
play. It was exciting to me, but even at that point I still didn't
think I was a writer, or that I could make a living writing. I
think that day finally came for me, as it does for all writers,
when you literally have to step out and address the sky. Go up
on a hill, or somewhere, preferably outside, and talk to the
sky and the wind and the elements. Say, "I'm a writer. I write.
That's what I do."

You make the declaration.

DC: That's right. It is a declaration. Absolutely. And it needs
to be said out loud. It's a commitment. It's a contract.

You make it sound like taking vows.

DC: You are taking vows. Exactly. There is a responsibility. To
me, it's like a religious calling. I grew up a Catholic, so I see
things in a particularly Catholic sort of way. I think the responsibility, the commitment, and the dedication is a calling.

What is the writer's responsibility?

DC: It is never to lie and never to deliberately hurt people.
However, if my father is an alcoholic, I have to write about

that. There's no two ways about it. Not hurting people does not mean shirking the truth. I think the writer is a mirror. The writer is a conscience for the public. He or she represents the truth. I believe my forte is characterization. I try to accurately and honestly portray people. I want my characters to be seen as survivors; people who endure. I'm doing a one-woman show I call *Women in the State of Grace.* It's about nine different women. I see my characters with their problems, their sadness, and their inadequacies. These people are doing the best they can with their lives. I try to portray them as accurately as I possibly can. I have a theater background. I work from the inside out, in much the same way as an actor or an actress works with their role. I try to work on my characterization and present it as clearly as I can.

Did you start out as an actress?
DC: I went to an all-girls Catholic high school. When I was a senior, I won a scholarship to major in drama at New Mexico State in Las Cruces, which I did for four years. There was a small group of people that did theater. I was in many of the plays. I did a lot of theater: Chekhov, Brecht, Beckett, Ionesco. You name it. I decided to go to graduate school in theater at Trinity University in San Antonio, Texas. I received an MFA. You might say I majored in play writing because in theater, you move from acting to directing to play writing. There are gradual steps. I think writers go through this training process too. You write poems, then you might write a short story, then a novel, or maybe a play. I think writers are always stretching themselves. In theater you do that as well. In school, I found myself writing more and acting less.

Are you teaching now?
DC: No, I'm not. Last year, I was a visiting writer in the creative writing department at New Mexico State. I went to the

University of New Mexico, and I wrote *The Last of the Menu Girls* as my master's thesis in creative writing.

Do you have any particular responsibility as a woman writer?
DC: Absolutely. Many of my characters are female. *The Menu Girls* is about the coming of age of a young woman in the Southwest. My new novel is called *Face of an Angel,* and it is about a career waitress. It's about the theme of service. What does it mean to serve and be served? Why are some people paid better and have an easier life? What is women's work, and why is it different from men's work? Why is it that we don't value women's service? This is a theme that interests me. Anyone who knows me or my work would say I'm a feminist writer. I'm a woman first. I'm a Chicana writer and a Latina writer. But I believe I'm also a universal writer. I would like to think I'm exploring the human heart, and that heart happens to be a female heart. I also have many male characters. I don't shy away from male characters. However, I think there are a lot of voices in my culture that have never been heard. I have a preface in my book that says, "My grandmother's voice was barely heard." These women were very soft spoken. Our grandmothers had no voices. They were workers. They were servers. My mother had a very difficult life. I remember her crying and moaning and carrying on. She was a teacher for forty-two years and had the varicose veins to prove it. She worked very hard. She was a single parent. She had a difficult life. These women never had a voice. I feel it's my responsibility to make a song of these voices. I live forty-two miles from the Mexican border, and it's important that I represent border images in this time of hysteria about immigration. We want to limit immigration, but these are the women

who clean our houses and take care of our children. What would we do without the workers that pick our food and clean our toilets? There are a lot of people that don't have a voice. I feel committed to my time and to my place, which is the desert. I try to represent my landscape, which I see as very feminine. I also try to represent the physical and spiritual aspects of God, which I also see as distinctly feminine. As a woman writer, I feel I'm tapping into these contemporary and ancestral voices.

Do you talk out loud when you write?
DC: Absolutely. I prance around. I carry my characters with me. A Dickens scholar once came up to me after a reading. He said, "You work very much in the manner of Charles Dickens." Apparently, Charles had mirrors in his studio. He would jump around when he worked. I write to a rhythm. I'm interested in the power of the paragraph and the flow of words. I'm also interested in the movement and the music of words. In a way all writers are musicians. I'm a musician. I'm a dancer.

Do you see the totality of art in writing and in words?
DC: Yes. I studied with Edward Albee in a play-writing class. He was a wonderful teacher, and I will forever be grateful to him because of the ideas he imparted to me. He said one should listen to the score of one's piece, even before setting it down in words. He worked out the music of his plays and of his characters before he wrote. When one starts to "perform," or to get the words out, there is enough material, enough substance within, to move the piece forward. I used to practice writing the alphabet. I talk about this in an essay called "Heat and Rain." It is important to have a certain manual dexterity as a writer. I've

always been interested in the "head to the heart to the hand" connection. I want it to be as fluid as possible. I write in longhand first, and then I move to the word processor. There is a certain physical workout that goes on in the creation of writing. When I write, I write very quickly. It takes me awhile to do the synthesis in my head. I think that's part of dancing. It's very exciting. In a way it's hard to talk about. You don't hear too many writers talk about the actual dance steps of writing, but there are many.

Is it a solo dance?

DC: No, not really. I enter into it with a sense of openness. As Rudolfo Anaya once said, "You let the wind and the spirits and the ancestors and your characters move through you. You are the transformer. You transmit the voices of these characters, but you do not let them damage you or hurt you." Many writers are damaged by their characters, as some actors are damaged by their characters. It's like the method actor who goes into a dark room and remembers the puppy that was killed. There's some part of that in writing, but I think of myself more as a person who plugs into this electrical socket, which is life and creativity. Yes, there is a certain amount of suffering or whatever that one goes through. It's there. It's accessible at all points. It's the dance. It's the music. It has nothing to do with that whole ego-obsessed world some writers carry around with them. It's the baggage of writing I want to do away with.

You're involved in so many things, and you have so many talents. How do you focus yourself?

DC: Before you called me, I was reading the *National Enquirer.* When I relax, I read and I lay there on my couch, and sometimes I fall asleep. I'm learning to relax more and to find joy in things like my family and working in the garden for a few hours in the evening. After I relax, I can come back to the characters. I've been stuck for about a week. I worked on a chapter, and it was very draining. I've just gone back to it today. I'm revising my novel. Sometimes you just have to take breaks from your work. I sleep and I read. I don't want to torture myself. When I write, I write very quickly. I can write a play in two weeks. That's because I've thought about the emotional life of the characters and the milieu they're going to inhabit. I've done my homework. To me, writing is an assemblage of parts. I don't sit down and say, "Okay, Act I, or Page 1." I know where I am by the time I get there, because I've worked through it in my notes and in my head. I write something every day. I am one of those persons who has pieces of paper all over the place. I'll write down "green tennis shoes," for example, and know it is a part of the puzzle that is the work. I'm always gathering.

The key is **always.** *A writer is* **always** *working.* **Always** *playing.*
DC: Yes. That's right. Writing is play. If we forget that spirit of play, it's very sad. Writing should be joyful.

Do you have a special environment where you write?
DC: I write everywhere. My husband is an artist, and he works at home. He's a sculptor and a jeweler, so he's always drilling on one side of the house. I have a workroom in the back where I have my computer. I was born in that room. It's very sacred to me. I work back in my birthroom. When I'm writing I become a lounge lizard. I might work in the living room. I move around when I'm writing the first draft. I'm restless. I have to move. As I become more contained and the work becomes more solidified, my space becomes smaller. Finally, I move to the room in the back. In the beginning, however,

I'm an animal that's going back and forth between spaces. Then, finally, the space becomes smaller, and I'm back in the place where I need to be.

Have you always lived in this house?
DC: I bought my house this year. It was a momentous and wonderful movement for me. I'm very happy that I own this house now. My mother passed away in 1983, and it took some time, but I finally bought it.

What advice do you give young writers in addition to your two rules? Is there anything you would do differently? Are there any mistakes?
DC: Sure, we've all made mistakes, but I don't look at it that way. We learn from things. I try to encourage writers to write about the things that move them passionately. Write about the things that have been crucial or elemental in your life. I have students make a list of what I call fifty "moments." Write about those wonderful things that have happened to you that make you who you are. Write about things like getting your first bra or the day your grandmother died. In a sense, it is gathering your own mythology. What are the stories that make up your whole myth as a person? I remember my mother telling about an uncle who was in a car accident. A wheel ran over his ear and chopped part of it off. That was part of our family's mythology. Every family has their myths and stories. Begin to make a list of the things that make you special and the things that have moved you. Try and work from that place of power. If you work from that honesty, I think the spirits will help you, and you will write stories that are free of ego. They may be a little awkward at first, but they'll be honest. These are the stories I hear from my students. These are the stories that can move people deeply. There was a police-

man in my class from New York who had never written before. He found the voice of his father who was an alcoholic. He was reading this story out loud, and he literally had a catharsis right then and there. He was able to become his father. That's the type of writing I'm interested in.

Are there any other excersises you recommend?

DC: I've learned a lot from monologues. I have my students write monologues. Write an ancestor monologue. Put yourself in the place of one of your ancestors. I'm working on a book of exercises for young people. It's called "Dear Juanita." This started when I received a letter from someone named Juanita. She said, "I want to be a writer." She spelled it "ritter." She asked "What do I do?" I gave her some exercises. I said, "Write a stranger monologue. Write about someone you know. Put yourself in the place of that person." You must write in the first person. Become this person. The monologue is a breakthrough for writers because it's about getting and holding the word as close to you as possible.

You refer to yourself as a performance writer. What does that mean?

DC: It comes from the cultural and the universal roots of storytelling. I come from a culture where if you're a good storyteller, you are valued. Writers should take speech courses. They should take acting courses. Writers should get up and speak. I go to poetry readings, and I'm bored to death. There's nothing happening. I hate to be bored. I come from a family where people sat around and told stories. The word, the "oral-ness" of stories is important. It's important to be able to move people and to make them laugh and sing and cry. The first actor was the storyteller sitting around the fire who got up and told a tale. I am a performance writer. I want to be someone whose stories are heard and told and remembered.

NIEN CHENG

NIEN CHENG was born in Beijing, China. She studied at the London School of Economics during the 1930s. There she met her husband, Kang-chi Cheng. The Chengs made their home in Shanghai, where Kang-chi served as general manager of Shell Oil Company. After her husband's death in 1957, Nien Cheng was hired by Shell as a special advisor. In 1966, Mao Zedong began the great proletarian cultural revolution. Later that year, Nien Cheng was arrested as "an enemy of the state" and imprisoned. She spent almost seven years in solitary confinement. Her daughter Meiping was murdered during this period. In 1976, Cheng was declared "rehabilitated," and a victim of wrongful arrest. She left China in 1980 and began writing *Life and Death in Shanghai* soon afterward. She lives in Washington, D.C.

Why do you write?
NC: I enjoy writing. I belong to the generation of people who used writing to communicate with each other. Even now, I prefer a letter to a phone conversation.

Why did you write your book? What steps led you to tell your amazing story?
NC: I wrote *Life and Death in Shanghai* in memory of my daughter Meiping. I was urged to write about my experience

during the cultural revolution by my old friends Peggy and Tillman Durdin, retired *New York Times* correspondents. By writing about what had happened, I also sorted out my memory of that time.

How did you remember so many details?
NC: I had to remember every little detail after each interrogation, especially the questions and the answers I gave. I knew the Communists often repeat the same questions later, sometimes a year later. If I did not give the same answers, they would accuse me of lying. I was brought up in the old way when a child was required to memorize whole essays. I started at the age of five to memorize Confucius's writings even though I did not understand the essays. I see scenes in my mind's eye when I talk about the past. I can't say I remember each little detail but certainly a lot more than people not required to memorize essays in their childhood years.

What can we learn from the lessons of history? What message do you hope the reader will take away from the tragic page in history you so eloquently describe in your book?
NC: The cultural revolution taught the Chinese people the folly of dictatorship and the need for democracy. This is good.

What is the writer's responsibility?
NC: In my opinion, the writer's responsibility is to tell the truth and to be objective.

It must be painful writing any type of autobiography, but especially one that includes an ordeal such as you experienced. Did you gain any insight into the experience by writing about it, and were you different in any way after you finished your book? Did you achieve any type of peace?

NC: It was painful to relive the past when I was writing *Life and Death in Shanghai.* Sometimes I had to put away the manuscript for weeks before returning to it to continue. After the book was finished, I felt good and more relaxed. I had fewer nightmares. But nothing can take away the sadness of losing my daughter.

Why is writing such a vital weapon against oppression?
NC: I suppose oppressors fear exposure.

Do you have any particular advice for young women?
NC: I think both men and women have a great deal to contribute to our world and make it a better place. I think most Americans are trying to do just that. This is a wonderful side of America and her real strength.

You are a very courageous woman. Is courage a necessary quality for a writer?
NC: I am not more courageous than others. When I was in prison, I was angry because I felt insulted that they said I was a spy. I think courage is important for everyone—both physical and moral courage.

What advice would you give the writer who aspires to write biography or even autobiography?
NC: To be truthful and honest and to be aware that writers have a responsibility to the readers.

Are you currently working on any projects?
NC: I only work on new projects sporadically. I want to write another book, but now I know too many people. They take up a lot of my time.

ANNIE DILLARD

*A*NNIE DILLARD was born in Pittsburgh, Pennsylvania. She graduated from Hollins College in Roanoke, Virginia, with a B.A. and later an M.A. in English. Dillard is an essayist, poet, and fiction writer. Her book *Pilgrim at Tinker Creek* won the Pulitzer Prize in 1975. Her non-fiction includes: *An American Childhood, The Writing Life, Tickets for a Prayer Wheel, Holy the Firm, Living by Fiction,* and *Teaching a Stone to Talk,* and a novel, *The Living.* Dillard is a writer in residence at Wesleyan University. She lives in Connecticut.

Why do you write?
AD: Why do I write? Like many writers', my writing is a fairly natural by-product of reading too much. The weeping sea mammals do something similar; their tears get rid of excess salt.

What are the differences and similarities between observing an urban landscape and a very natural and rustic environment? What tools should the writer use to detect subtle contrasts and details in all life?
AD: Writing a story set in a city uses the same processes as writing a story set in the country, just as drawing a building uses the same processes as drawing a tree. You keep your story's point in mind, and you pay attention—in writing, to the

imagined and remembered scene, and in drawing to the actual scene.

Why did you select the quote from Emerson, "No one suspects the days to be gods," to open The Writing Life?
AD: Why did I begin *The Writing Life* with a certain quotation from Emerson? Emerson wrote in a letter to his dear friend Margaret Fuller, "No one suspects the days to be gods." This theme interests me. A favorite book called *Holy the Firm*—a nonfiction narrative—explores it. In the writing life, as in all life, thinking of the days as gods hallows the days, and makes more real to the imagination the possibility of their significance. There are, of course, many kinds of gods.

People's lives are so cluttererd today with all kinds of stimuli. How should a writer strip down her life in order to achieve the state of mind and the discipline necessary to write?
AD: You ask how writers can avoid the clutter of too much stimulus. Writers differ, and many writers like to, and need to, keep up with current events and trends. Those who don't can throw away the sources of the noise. Their friends will forgive them for living singularly.

The Writing Life *contains a kind of urgency in sentences such as "Write as if you were dying," and "I do not so much write a book as sit up with it, as with a dying friend." Could you elaborate on these ideas?*
AD: You quote *The Writing Life:* "I do not so much write a book as sit up with it, as with a dying friend." Like much of *The Writing Life,* this is a joke. I hold the writing's hand, in dread and sympathy for its many disorders. "Write as if you were dying" is another joke. You're dying. I can't really rec-

ommend *The Writing Life,* though the jokes still tickle me. The rest of it seems both too strong and too trivial.

What is the most important advice you offer young writers?
AD: You ask what advice I offer young writers. If they ask, I encourage them to keep reading for pleasure.

RITA DOVE

*R*ITA DOVE held the prestigious honor of being the poet laureate of the United States for 1993. In 1987, she became one of the youngest writers to win the Pulitzer Prize for poetry, and she was also the second African-American to win this award. Rita Dove was born and raised in Akron, Ohio. Her books of poetry include *Grace Notes, Museum, Thomas and Beulah,* and *The Yellow House on the Corner.* She has written a play entitled *The Darker Face of the Earth,* as well as a collection of short stories, *Fifth Sunday,* and a novel, *Through the Ivory Gate.* Dove is the recipient of a fellowship from the National Endowment for the Arts and the Guggenheim Foundation. She is a professor of English at the University of Virginia, and she lives in Charlottesville with her husband and daughter.

Why do you write?
RD: I can't answer this question; or rather I've been asking myself the same question ever since I took up a pen and first made up a story.

When did you first become aware of your desire to write?
RD: Ah, this is easier to answer. I began writing around the age of nine or ten. By that I mean I voluntarily composed stories in my free time, rather than waiting for a teacher to assign "creative writing" as part of a language arts unit. My

first writings were variations on comic books (I specialized in female protagonists/super heroines) and with my older brother, devised a neighborhood newspaper during the summer.

The language of your novel is very musical. Is there a connection between the language of poetry and the language of the novel?
RD: Of course there is a connection between the language of the two genres; after all, language is the medium used in each. Although my intention when writing the novel was to make it as much a work of prose as possible, I also believe that a good fiction writer is as deeply aware of the possibilities of the compressed languages as the best of our poets.

Do you feel any particular responsibility toward African-American women, or women in general, in how you portray your characters?
RD: No. I do not. My only responsibility is toward the truth as it appears in that particular moment; I also feel a commitment to the felicities and possibilities of language. I believe that the artist cannot swerve in his or her dedication to the art in order to satisfy the preconceived notions of any group or political movement.

Are you disciplined? How do you structure your time, and how do you organize your writing process?

RD: My chief disciplining agent is a highly developed sense of guilt. Although I do tend to be moderately organized, and I also set aside specific hours per week to write, this schedule is a flexible one due to the exigencies of daily life with its shifting responsibilities—parenting, teaching, general emergencies, and the like. When my daughter goes to school, I try to reserve those hours for writing, since I am assured of relatively uninterrupted quiet. Of course, the demands of answering correspondence, teaching, and public appearances can throw a week's schedule out of joint; in those instances, my personal sense of guilt sends me to the desk at any hour of the day or night.

Do you have any particular advice for youing writers?
RD: My first and really only piece of advice is to read, read, read. One cannot call oneself a writer if one does not love the other end of that trajectory. Also, through reading anything one can get one's hands on—from the back of cereal boxes to Plato's *The Republic*—the young writer learns to open his or her mind to the possibilities of using language to articulate our most complicated emotions.

FANNY FLAGG

*F*ANNY FLAGG was born in Birmingham, Alabama. Her first writing venture was a three-act comedy entitled *The Whoopee Girls*. She also directed, produced, and starred in the production. She was in the fifth grade. By entering the Miss Alabama contest, Flagg won a scholarship to the Pittsburgh Playhouse. Flagg began writing and producing television specials at the age of nineteen. She has appeared in more than five hundred television shows (including "Candid Camera") as well as motion pictures and stage productions. She is the author of *Fried Green Tomatoes at the Whistle Stop Cafe*. She also co-authored the 1991 screenplay with Carol Sobieski; both were nominated for an Academy Award for screenwriting. Flagg is also the author of *Daisy Fay and the Miracle Man*. She lives in California.

Why do you write?
FF: I'm not sure, but I think it is because I was not happy with the true facts of life. I wanted to create a world I understood and I could control, where I could express the admiration I have for ordinary people who just live their lives in a quiet and noble way and never get or expect any rewards for it.

At what point did you realize you wanted to write, and what form did your words take?
FF: I was in the fifth grade and I wrote a play. It was a comedy

called *The Whoopee Girls*. It starred myself and my best friend.

Were you particularly influenced by Southern writers such as Eudora Welty or Flannery O'Connor or any other writers?
FF: I was particularly influenced by Tennessee Williams' plays such as *The Glass Menagerie*. It affected me greatly. I was also influenced by Eudora Welty, Truman Capote, John Steinbeck, William Kennedy, Donald Hall, and Garrison Keillor.

Is **Fried Green Tomatoes** *in any way autobiographical?*
FF: It is based loosely on my Great Aunt Bess who ran a café in the thirties. *Daisy Fay and the Miracle Man* is more autobiographical than *Fried Green Tomatoes*.

Are you disciplined? Describe how you conquer writer's block if this is ever a problem for you.
FF: I am not disciplined in the sense that I write every day. I may not write at all for three or four years at a time, but when I do, I am excited, and I write every day if I can.

How does your acting background affect you as a writer?
FF: Because I was an actress and I know comedy, I have a certain rhythm in my head. I can hear the words spoken as well as see them written. Timing is important, and I think my dialogue is already edited down to its shortest form because I know and listen to how real people speak. My experience working with "Candid Camera" was invaluable.

Please describe how you felt to be nominated for an Academy Award in screenwriting?
FF: I was thrilled, but the joy was somewhat tempered with great disappointment that the actresses and the director of the film did not receive nominations as well.

Is it difficult making the switch from novelist to screenwriter?
FF: It is very hard to break down a 400-page book with more than 150 characters, and that spans a period of over eight years, into 120 pages. Telling as much of the story in approximately 1 1/2 hours of screen time is very hard. I was fortunate to have a partner and a director who were devoted to getting this movie made.

Fried Green Tomatoes *contains four strong women characters. Do you think women have a responsibility in how they portray women?*
FF: I think any writer has a responsibility to portray men and women as truthfully and as compassionately as possible. I try to see the best in people and understand why people who do act in a negative way are only crying out for love or out of pain. I believe we write to enlighten and educate and try to ask the reader to "walk a moment in another's shoes," so to speak. We also try to entertain and allow the reader to lose themselves in another world for a while and hopefully gain some insight into people different from themselves.

Do you have any particular advice for aspiring novelists or screen-writers?
FF: I have the same advice you can get at a railroad crossing: Stop . . . look . . . and listen. Don't write until you have something to say and you cannot hold it back any longer.

Could you describe your writing environment? Are you neat?
FF: My writing environment is a mess. I like to come to work in the morning to a neat room, but as the day goes on, papers are everywhere. Because of that, I like to work in a big empty room with wooden floors, so at the end of the day I can just sweep the floor so I can have a clean room the next day.

PAULA GUNN ALLEN

*P*AULA GUNN ALLEN is the daughter of a Laguna Pueblo, Sioux, and Scottish mother and a Lebanese-American father. She was born in New Mexico and is one of the foremost Native American literary critics. She is the author of *Skins and Bones* and six additional volumes of poetry. She is also the author of a novel, *The Woman Who Owned the Shadows*. Her book *The Sacred Hoop: Recovering the Feminine in American Indian Traditions* represents a major contribution to both feminist and American Indian scholarship. Paula Gunn Allen is also the editor of two anthologies: *Studies in American Indian Literature* and *Spider Woman's Granddaughters: Native American Women's Traditional and Short Stories*. She is the recipient of grants from the National Endowment for the Arts and The Ford Foundation. Her most recent work includes *Grandmothers of the Light: A Medicine Woman's Sourcebook* and the two volume set, *Voice of the Turtle: A Century of American Indian Fiction*. Paula Gunn Allen is a professor of Native American studies at the University of California at Los Angeles.

Why do you write?
PGA: Beats me. I don't know. I smoke, but I can't figure out why I smoke. Maybe they're similar.

If you stopped smoking do you think you would stop writing?
PGA: I doubt it. I stopped smoking once, but I didn't stop writing.

Do you mean to say that writing is like a habit?
PGA: Yes. It's something I started doing in adolescence and never stopped. A lot of the things I write, I write because someone has asked me. It might be a sort of feminine thing I do to please other people. It happens that I've become pretty influential in the process. I often wonder if I might not be happier if I just quit.

Why? Does writing make you unhappy?
PGA: Writing is very difficult. Any writer will tell you that. It's painful. I'll balance my checkbook rather than get to work. Although I must say, since menopause writing is not only easier, but a great deal more enjoyable. I don't know why. I do know one thing, however: my mind has cleared up enormously. It isn't that my thoughts weren't clear before; it's that now I somehow know things in a way that feels very secure and sure. Things I wondered about for a long time seem to have snapped into focus. It's a very odd thing, and I certainly wasn't expecting it. Nobody told me this would happen.

At least that's something positive. It's about time we hear something positive about menopause.
PGA: Even though my body is deteriorating, my mind is getting stronger and stronger. And writing has become more and more fun.

What is the hardest part about writing? Is it the beginning?
PGA: Yes. The hardest part is getting what I call a "handle."

I might spend months, maybe years, doing something I call "mumbling around in my head." I used to kid my mother about talking around the edges. I do that too. It drives my students nuts. When I write, publishers and editors get really annoyed because I tend to suggest, rather than say things directly. I do this sort of mumbling around the edges until I get some sense of the direction. It's not really content and it isn't exactly structure. Once I get an approach, or I know what the direction is, then I can work. Before that I'm making notes or I'm just thinking. I also read a lot in the general area of whatever it is that interests me. I just wrote a long piece about nuclear power and radiation. I had been thinking about the subject for ten years, and I had given some lectures about it in which I incorporated some ideas and reflections. I was primarily interested in the Native American relationship to this stuff, partly because it's on Indian land. The first uranium that was used for the first bombs was found on my reservation. It was found near a place that my great-grandmother used to tell a story about. You know how your intuition puts things together? I didn't know what my intuition was noticing, but when I began to write, I understood that those two things were connected. That was all there was to it. All I had to do was explore the connection. That was easy. It took me a long time to notice what was in my mind. That's the hardest part.

Is that the struggle?
PGA: Yes, that's the struggle. Education makes our mind want to go in directions that have already been explored. The linear aspect of the mind, the part that goes to school, that reads and writes doesn't want to go around the edges,

but a writer needs to be aware of the edges and to power-
fully connect with them *on the page.*

Isn't that the writer's role, to go beyond?
PGA: Exactly. The writer's role is to lead the reader into
different ways of looking at things.

*You mentioned that you started writing as an adolescent. What
kinds of things did you write?*
PGA: The first thing I wrote was what I call a "hysterical"
love story. I was fourteen. I recently saw a Doris Day movie,
and it was really repulsive. When I was twelve it wasn't
repulsive. It was absolutely beautiful. I wanted to be Doris
Day.

Did you also write poetry?
PGA: I wrote some poetry when I was in college. I was pretty good at it. I didn't do anything for a while after that. I
got married, and then I got the "Famous Writer's Course."
It was very good, but unfortunately I couldn't keep it up.
There were a lot of reasons. I was very poor, and I had two
babies. As a consequence of the writer's course, however, I
finally noticed I had an interest, and I sort of fell into a
poetry class with Robert Creeley at the University of New
Mexico. After that, I thought of myself as a poet and a
writer.

*When I read Native American literature I often expect to find a
lot of anger—justifiable anger—but instead I find enormous
spiritual strength.*
PGA: I'm glad you said that. I was at a Third World writer's
conference in Sacramento in 1982. It was absolutely fascinating. There must have been ninety different sessions.
There was so much anger in the poetry, and yet every time

an Indian got on stage, they read spiritual poetry. I knew all the Native poets, and I knew that we had all written some really enraged poetry. What was fascinating to me, however, was that it wasn't like everyone got together and said, "Okay, let's be spiritual." It was entirely random. I wrote an article about it because I became very interested in why this happened. Spirituality marks Native work and makes it very distinct from any other work being written in this country.

Why is Native writing spiritual?

PGA: Native writers include spirituality in such a way that it's embedded in a regular story. It's embedded in a poetical discussion. It's embedded in life itself. It's not, "Oh, the noble Indian." It's not that kind of new-age stuff. It's very tightly connected. In the traditional way, spiritual life is completely embedded in the practical life. You can see this reflected in the literature of Native people.

Is this spirituality one reason there's been such a renewed interest in Native literature? Do people have a need?

PGA: Yes. There's this tremendous hunger. I must also say that Native writers are good. They're really good. I've had graduate assistants tell me that when they've used a Native story or two in their freshman comp classes, the oddest thing has happened. Because students generally don't like freshman comp, they'd sit there half asleep. When they'd get to the Native story, however, they'd all wake up. The students would get really excited, and they'd write really good papers. They wanted more. That tells me there's something happening in those stories that is especially important to young people. But what that something is, I don't know.

Why do you think it has taken so long for this work to be read by a mass audience?

PGA: Racism. Flat out racism. It's complex and it's very difficult. The racism has worked in two ways. For one thing, some American publishers, editors, and critics don't want to see the work because they've already decided we're savages. They've "known" that (ho ho) for a very long time. It's only since the sixties that people decided, "Wait a minute, that's probably not the case." People in power have begun to rethink their attitudes. So that's one part of it. The other part is that when you've been as tremendously devastated as we have—we lost some ninety-six percent of our population during the Anglo-European take over— you're not in a powerful psychological condition to argue with an established alien group and get them to notice you. You don't want anything to do with them. So the racism is operating in two directions.

Do you think attitudes are changing?

PGA: Yes, but there's still a lot of arguing. I never send out a piece that I don't have to argue.

What do you argue about?

PGA: For example, the editors may not like the way my work is put together. They want a white piece with feathers. They don't want it to say any number of things that they don't think fits "Indians." They don't want it to be structured like a Native work. They don't like Native structures because they can't follow them. They want all the transitions clear. They want it logical and linear. They get bored and say, "Oh, it's only about Indians." I've actually had editors say things like that. It's not just me; I've talked with other Native writers. It's everywhere. Our stories are often seen as science fiction, while we think of them as being about ordinary life. Editors say, "That's science fiction, and we don't publish science fiction." It's extraordinarily difficult. The miracle is that we are getting published. This is due in large part to the small presses. And as a result of their support, a lot of the major presses have picked up on Native work because of the success of the small presses.

In your book, **The Sacred Hoop,** *you describe incredibly strong Native women. Why have western cultures often portrayed women as weak and helpless?*
PGA: Official Christianity fixed it that way. Women have an image that they can't develop their own sense of inner power, inner strength, and inner security. When you can't develop (or show) your strength because the symbols of your culture tell you you can't, you never develop those traits to begin with. Most little girls in patriarchal systems learn very quickly at home and in school settings that they are not important. That message gets internalized very quickly. It's not at the verbal level, so when you grow up you can't effectively deal with it because it doesn't have words. In Native cultures that doesn't happen. There is a lot of fighting, and certainly men put down women and women put down men. There's a kind of balance, however, because that inner sense of female strength isn't being messed with. It's developing.

There are so many amazing women writers that are never taught in school. There are also a great many strong women in history that we never hear about.
PGA: It makes me mad. Why didn't we know? Why were we deprived? It enrages me. I was in my forties when I discovered the poet H.D., or Hilda Doolittle. Although I had

majored in literature and minored in creative writing, I had only seen two of her worst poems. Finally I discovered H.D. through a friend. I was angry because if I'd had H.D. as a model when I was in college, that awareness would have increased my ability as a writer. H.D. was the kind of model I needed. Instead, I wound up trying to model myself after white male writers, and they weren't doing what I really needed. William Carlos Williams came close, but H.D. was *it*. So there I was in my forties before I discovered her. I was so angry.

What projects are you working on now?
PGA: I just finished the first volume of a two-volume anthology about American Indian fiction from the turn of the century until the nineties. That's almost a hundred years. I'm also working on an encyclopedia of American Indian goddesses, supernaturals, and heroines. Additionally, I'm doing a children's book of Native biographies with a friend. And for myself, I'm working on a suite of sonnets. I'm really having fun.

Is it important to have this balance in your work?
PGA: Yes. It's very important. I have a tendency to put off doing the things I love. I'm more motivated by what others want. If someone calls and says, "Will you do such and such?" Instead of saying, "Well, I'd like to, but I'm writing a novel and some poems," I say, "Okay." My own work then gets put aside. I've just had a year off. I've written three essays I really enjoyed. They were just for me.

Native literature talks about the connection between human beings and nature. This seems to imply a kind of tolerance.
PGA: That depends on how you define tolerance.

As an acceptance of all living things?

PGA: Yes. Tolerance in the liberal white world tends to mean, "I tolerate you." That is very different from, "I acknowledge and respect you. My being depends on your being. I know this and therefore I honor you."

SUE GRAFTON

SUE GRAFTON is one of the most widely read mystery writers in the 1990s. She is the author of thirteen novels. Her "Kinsey Millhone" mysteries, *"A" Is for Alibi* through *"K" Is for Killer,* have been published worldwide. Grafton is also the author of numerous short stories and essays. Among her screenwriting credits are the screenplay *Lolly–Madonna XXX,* as well as nine teleplays and numerous episodes for television series. She is a frequent lecturer and has won many awards for her writing. Grafton was born in Louisville, Kentucky, and graduated from the University of Louisville. She is married to the writer Steven Humphrey. Grafton is the mother of three children.

Why do you write?

SG: I don't think it's possible to answer the question about why I write. My father, C.W. Grafton, was a municipal bond attorney in Louisville, Kentucky, where I was born and raised. He was also a writer and published three mysteries in the course of his career: *The Rat Began to Gnaw the Rope, The Rope Began to Hang the Butcher,* and *Beyond a Reasonable Doubt.* His first mystery novel, *The Rat Began to Gnaw the Rope,* won the Mary Roberts Rinehart Award of 1943. Because of him, I not only became a writer, but I developed a real passion for the mystery genre.

Did you always want to write mysteries, or did your writing take other forms when you were younger?

SG: Writing was my obsession long before it occurred to me that I could make a living at it. In both junior high school and high school, I worked on the school paper. I started writing short stories when I was eighteen and completed my first novel when I was twenty-two years old. It took me four completed, full-length manuscripts before I had a book accepted for publication. I was twenty-five at the time. From the age of twenty-two on, I wrote at night, every night, while I was working full time as a medical secretary and raising a family. I had two mainstream novels published in my twenties: *Keziah Dane* and *The Lolly–Madonna War.* The film rights for *Lolly–Madonna War* were purchased by a British film producer, whom I collaborated with on the film script. That film came out in 1973. After that, I spent many years in Hollywood writing movies for television, solo at first, and then in collaboration with my husband, Steven Humphrey.

What have you learned about yourself through your writing and through your central character, Kinsey Millhone?

SG: Kinsey Millhone is my alter ego . . . the person I might have been had I not married young and had children. I think of us as one soul in two bodies, and she got the good one. The 1968 VW she drove (until *"G" Is for Gumshoe*) was a car I owned some years ago. In *"H" Is for Homicide,* she acquires the 1974 VW that's sitting out behind my house. It's pale blue with only one minor ding in the left rear fender. (I don't mind her driving the car, but with her driving record I refuse to put her on my insurance policy.) I own both hand guns she talks about and, in fact, I learned to shoot so that I'd know what it felt like. I own the all-purpose dress she refers to. I've also been married and divorced twice, though to different men. I finally got it right and I'm now married to husband number three, whom I expect to be with for life. What's interesting about her presence in my life is that I lead, in essence, two lives . . . hers and mine. Because of her, I've taken a women's self-defense class and a class in criminal law. I've also made the acquaintance of doctors, lawyers, P.I.s, cops, coroners, all manner of experts.

Is there anything strikingly different about you and Kinsey?
SG: Kinsey and I have different biographies; different life lines, in effect. But our observations of the world, our attitudes, and many (though not all) of our opinions are the same. Since I'm not a private investigator, and since I have no background in law enforcement, I have to do copious research in order to have the sort of casual, throwaway information that Kinsey would have at her disposal as a matter of course. She can only "know" what I know so I consider it my responsibility to make sure she knows the right stuff. The trick is doing it so smoothly that the reader doesn't spot the effort. To the reader, it should feel like, "Well, of course she'd know that . . . any good detective would . . ."

How did you learn about murder, weapons, and all the data necessary to write mysteries?
SG: When I started work on *"A" Is for Alibi,* I wasn't even sure what a private investigator did. In the process of writing that first book, I began the long and continuing task of educating myself. I studied forensics, toxicology, books on burglary and theft, homicide, arson, anatomy, poisonous plants, etc.

Describe your writing environment.
SG: I write in an office in my home in Santa Barbara. My windows look out across our very green and serene formal garden toward the mountains. The office itself is done in mauve and white, and I make every attempt to keep it exceedingly neat. The creative process is so chaotic that I find it distressing to be surrounded by clutter and disorder. I have good light, my word processor, a

library of reference books, my files, a few much loved objects in my immediate surroundings, a comfortable chair with a good floor lamp by it, four plants, an ecosphere which contains three brine shrimp and a snail. On the wall is a framed blowup of the cover of *"G" Is for Gumshoe,* the first hardback that made the *New York Times* best-sellers list, and a photograph of me as a six-month-old sitting on my mother's lap, looking up at her adoringly while my sister, who was three, stands nearby, grinning at the camera.

How has success changed you, your writing habits, or your work?
SG: Success hasn't changed me in any essential way. My stress levels go up periodically because I have such a high profile these days. I'm constantly being asked to do public-speaking engagements, most of which I refuse. I feel my time and energy belong to the books. I'm also bored with the sound of my own voice, and I find I'm not interested in being *the entertainment* for the groups who seek my services. I have enough money now to do as I please and go where I want to go. What I find is that, for the most part, I want to be here in Santa Barbara, doing my work. I consider the task I've undertaken a spiritual journey, and I strive every day of my life to understand how to do what I've set out to do. I'm very clear about what I want, what I'm willing to do, and what I'm not willing to do. I try to eliminate anything that doesn't pertain. My life is filled with my family, my writing, exercise, reading, and a few good friends. What I love about the mystery is that I know I'll never conquer the form.

Do you have any particular advice for aspiring writers?
SG: My advice for those interested in writing is as follows: You need to read as much as possible, learn to spell correctly, and rewrite incessantly. I never turn in a book without redoing every sentence at least three times. Anything else is sloppy work in my opinion. I feel most "novice" writers are too attentive to the ques-

tion of how to get an agent and how to get published and not nearly attentive enough to the matter of learning their craft. In my experience, if you aren't passionate about the *process* of writing, you'd be better advised to try something else. Writing is a mirror we hold up to our own faces day after day. Most people don't have the courage or the strength of character to look at what's really there. Most of us spend our lives trying to avoid criticism, refusing to take risks, and pretending to be something we're not. None of this is possible when you devote your life to writing. It's not for the fainthearted or the impatient, and egotists need not apply. Writing is a holy mission; not something you do, but something you are. It is as much the defining principle of my life as religion might be to somebody else.

Do you recommend any particular books for aspiring writers?
SG: I have several that I recommend. Three are by Lawrence Block: *Writing the Novel: From Plot to Print* and *Spider, Spin Me a Web*, and *Telling Lies for Fun and Profit*. I'm also impressed with *The Mystery Writers Handbook, Writing Suspense and Mystery Fiction*, and Patricia Highsmith's *Plotting and Writing Suspense Fiction*. In 1992, I was asked to edit *Writing Mysteries*, a new anthology of essays on crime writing by some of the finest mystery writers working in the field today. The chapters are arranged so that the novice mystery writer can "walk through" the process of writing a mystery novel, from that first spark of an idea, to research, character development, plotting, outlining, and execution, culminating in marketing suggestions once the book is completed.

Do you have a favorite quotation about writing?
SG: I like to keep in mind a Eudora Welty quotation: "Every novel teaches you the lessons necessary to write that book." She goes on to remark that the only problem is that the lessons don't really carry over from one work to the next. Oh, darn.

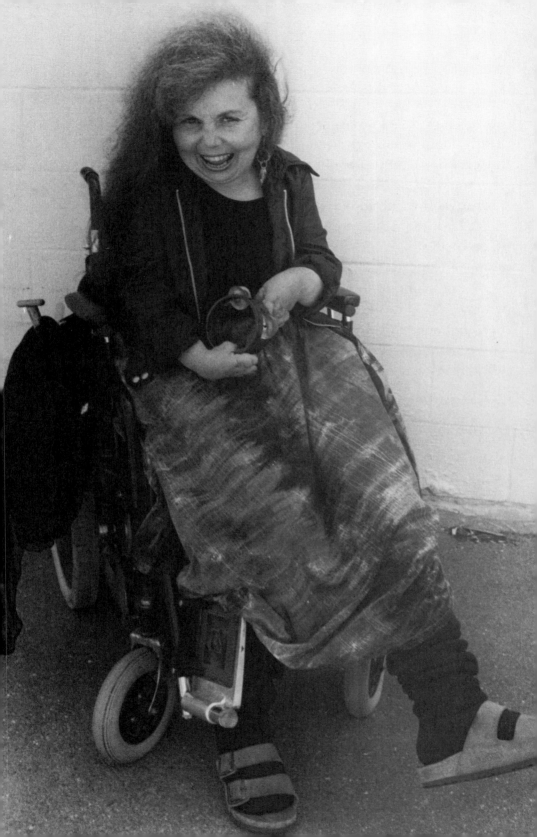

CHERYL MARIE WADE

CHERYL MARIE WADE is a poet and performance artist. Her theater piece *A Woman With Juice* had its premiere at BRAVA! For Women in the Arts as part of San Francisco's prestigious Solo Mio performance art festival. Other performance works by Cheryl Marie Wade include *Sassy Girl, Dylan Concert Collage, Disability Culture Rap,* and *Here.* The video she produced of *Here* garnered five awards and earned her the Ce Ce Robinson Award for artistic achievement. She was grand prize winner of the 1991 Oakland Poetry Joust, director of WRY CRIPS Disabled Women's Theater Group, and an original member of AXIS Dis/Abled Dance Troupe. Cheryl Marie Wade has been published in such journals as *Calyx, Ikon, Woman of Power,* the *Disability Rag,* and *Ms.,* and she edits a series of anthologies for Squeaky Wheels Press, featuring the creative work of people with disabilities. She serves on the board of the Corporation on Disabilities and Telecommunications and was honored as one of the Outstanding Women of Berkeley by the Commission on the Status of Women. She has B.A. and a master's degrees in Psychology from the University of California. Cheryl Marie Wade lives in Berkeley, California.

Why do you write?
CMW: Writing was always something I loved. Even as a child, I was very verbal and I loved words. The joke in my family was

that when I asked my mother what my first word was, she'd say I didn't have one. I had a first monologue. I think I was preordained or predestined to be involved with language. I always had a very active imagination which was partly fueled by the fact that I come from a very dysfunctional family. It was a survival tool. I needed to create some kind of life in my head. As I became more disabled, I started keeping a journal. I am also a sexual abuse survivor. Writing was one of the ways I kept my sanity. I had another life. Writing was a way of keeping myself whole and a way of finding some kind of identity. That was a big part of writing. I created "Cheryl, the Hero" in my journal, and I had a great life.

Did writing help you gain confidence in yourself?
CMW: Working on the issues of sexual abuse and coming to terms with my body was a big step. I didn't always have confidence. When I first went back to school around 1974, I carried a shawl in my lap to hide my hands. That's how far I've come. Being involved politically in the disability rights movement has also helped. A lot of times I hated my body, but I got behind the issue and I said, "All right, just because you're in a wheelchair doesn't mean you shouldn't be able to get into a building or be able to participate in a program." On an intellectual level, I connected with politics, and that gave me something to hook into and fight for. The more I was out there, and the more I spoke out politically, the more I was able to feel power as a person. This power didn't really come together for me personally until I started to analyze my body. I sort of picked it apart and wrote about both the ugly side and the power of the differences. Once I was able to be out in the world more, I found people listened to me. I put myself in situations where I was afraid, but I pushed my way

through. I was intelligent and articulate, and that made me feel I had power. By writing about my body and about what I call the "ugly beauty" of disability, I began to like my body. I do mind the pain and the limitations, but I don't hate the actual physical differences anymore.

How did you discover this power?
CMW: I realized that my hands have a lot of power. People are drawn to my body. Although they are usually drawn to the negatives, I worked with that and turned it into a powerful thing. I took all the negatives about the word "deformity" and turned them around. There's power in being different. I learned to work with my disability. I learned not to make it my enemy. It is my partner and a part of my art. I began to look at the power of it and the fact that it has a positive aspect.

What you're really talking about is acceptance. Don't you think it's difficult for people to accept who they are?
CMW: I watched some of these talk shows while I was recuperating from my operation. There are so many women who start out looking fine and then have numerous surgeries to make themselves look "better." When I went back to school, the first thing I wanted to do was save money for breast implants. It wasn't really my breasts that were the problem. It was my whole image of myself. I didn't like the fact that I was a disabled person, and I didn't think I was attractive. I put my frustration on my small breasts, because I couldn't do anything about my hands or my legs. Fortunately, it took so long to raise enough money, that by the time I had the money, I didn't want to have breast implants. I bought a van instead; I figured it would take me farther. I see these women who are,

in traditional terms, far more acceptable to the outside world than I am. I see them spending thousands of dollars trying to have large breasts, a tight butt, thin thighs, a flat stomach, and a perfect nose, and I realize it all comes from not valuing who you are. Somewhere along the line it occurred to me that I'm a very valuable person. I received a lot of validation for my wit. People always told me I was funny. And again, I kept that little journal where I was the hero. I kept some kind of ego intact by saying that Cheryl was a whole person. I kept saying this, even though there was very little in my life at the time that indicated it was true. This was just something I believed. Once I had the opportunity to be in the world and to express who I really was, I got the validation that it was in fact true.

How is writing a means for validation?
CMW: A lot of it is discovery. I discover so much when I write. When I wrote my first poem about hands: "Mine are the hands of your bad dreams . . . Booga Booga," I didn't know I felt any of those things. I didn't know I felt strong enough to poke fun at people's fears of my body's differences. I realized there was an enormous change from the person holding a shawl to hide her hands to the person able to shake her hands on stage and say, "Booga Booga." I knew there was something very powerful in that transformation.

How do you use humor to get across a very strong message?
CMW: One of the things I notice with humor is that it's a great icebreaker. The kind of humor I do is not necessarily apologetic. I'm not one of those people who makes fun of my disability. I make fun of the trappings of disability. I don't make fun of the way my hands look. I don't make fun of my

body. I don't make fun of what I can't do. What I do make fun of is the way people react to me. I poke fun at the goofiness of our society and the barriers. I make fun of the stereotypes. It's what I call "vicious humor," and it does break the barrier. If someone can laugh with you, and if you can control what they're laughing at, you will open them up. Laughter opens up the airways, or the brain, or the heart, or whatever. It lets in the heavier stuff. There's a lot of pain in my humor. I don't have any problems with blowing images away. If you can look at me and say, "Oh, disabled people actually have a sense of humor," that's great. Usually we're looked upon as tragic victims. Most of the disabled people I know have an outrageous sense of humor.

Tell me about using the music of your wheelchair in your performance piece.

CMW: Several years ago I was working with a group of disabled women, and we started playing around with the idea that we made interesting noises. People who walk on crutches, people who have canes, and people with power wheelchairs make very interesting noises. Sometimes you enter a room and you just want to die because everyone looks at you. There's the sound of these big motors and the sound of the wheels rubbing on the floor. I thought, "Okay, here's another thing I can use." You hear this clickity-click. It's percussion. The wheels make a sound. It's music. If you can work with that, it gives you another tool as a performer. I can't play the guitar, but I can play my wheelchair. I play it every day. I think my poetry is somewhat affected by the rhythm of my chair and the sound of my computer. I was raised on rock and roll. Using my chair in this way is one of the things that's received the most response. People ask, "How did you decide to use your chair as an instrument?" It's always by accident. A lot of what art is, is an accident. It's all about the moment of discovery. For the writer or the performer, something clicks and you keep it. You say, "Oh, that works," and you grab it and refine it.

How is your writing inspired? Do you work in spurts?
CMW: Yes. It does come in spurts. There's no doubt about it. I'm not one of those prolific writers who sits down every day and writes or keeps a very accurate journal. I tried that, but it didn't work very well for me. My journals are so boring when I sit down and say, "I will write something every day." So I just gave up on that. Now I write while I'm sitting in the waiting room at the doctor's office or sitting out on my back porch listening to the sound of the wind and the birds. Once, when I was feeling very sad because my favorite relative had died, I wrote a piece about the spirit of that person. Things like that hit me very intensely and emotionally. I've gotten a lot of my poetry from dreams. I'll wake up in the middle of the night with a line. The line "Club Foot Annie wearing bright red shoes" came to me during the night. I woke up, and I wrote it down in my notebook. A lot of my poems come that way. I'll get an image and write it down even though I may not know where it's going. My best work comes from an image I might have in a dream. All of a sudden an image will come, and I'll write it down. I feel my least effective poems come from thought. These are sometimes the poems the publishers are more interested in. But as a performer, the most effective poems come from images. I start with an image or a very strong emotion, and it flows from there. I'm not a very prolific writer. Some of my poems have taken two or three years. I don't sit down and say, "Whamo, here's a poem." It's like me.

I'm a work in progress. Writing is a discovery. If I'm writing, it might take awhile to figure out where I want to go with the poem. A lot of times a poem will come from a feeling. For example, one of the poems that has received the most response is a poem called "I am not one of." One day I sat down and started writing images in my book. I wrote line after line of "Who am I?" I was depressed. I felt demoralized. It was almost like an exercise. I wrote down everything I could think of: "I'm not a euphemism. I'm not an easy euphemism to make you feel comfortable. I'm not 'physically challenged.' I'm a tougher image than that." There are all these euphemisms. I hate expressions like "physically challenged." They might make some people feel more comfortable, but they aren't about reality. So what I did was counterpoint these ideas. If I'm not that, what am I? "I'm a sock in the eye with gnarled fist." Some of these images come from the history of disability. We were the first victims of the Holocaust. Very few people know that. Mental and physical "defectives" were used for special treatment programs. It was through the treatment of disabled and mentally disabled people that the Nazis got their ideas of torture. Without first sanctioning the horrible treatment of disabled people, they would never have gone on to the Jews. That's the way I look at it. What could happen to us, what could happen to the most vulnerable in society, will eventually happen to others. If you don't stop it here, look out. That's where the poems come from. They come from everything I've soaked in and everything I've ever read about disability. And, of course, from being female.

Do you have any advice for getting started as a writer?
CMW: Find an ally. Find an ally to write or talk with. Some dis-

abled people can't write. Get a tape recorder. If you have a verbal disability and you can't talk very well, get a stick and type your words onto a typewriter or a computer. There's a lot of wonderful technology that can free the voices of people who don't have the power of their hands, or of their movement. You have to be assertive and you have to fight for things. It's the only way. Find an ally and figure out what it is you want to do and then push for that. Push people. Say to them, "I need this. I want this." Tell them what would make you happy. Tell them what would give you the juice in life. Don't be afraid to make mistakes. People think they have to be brilliant the first time they do something. If you think that way you'll never do anything. The first time you pick up a pen and write a poem it will be dumb. If you think you're going to be a poet the first time you write something, think again. I'm a firm believer in submitting your work to small presses. There are a lot of places for beginners. There's nothing quite like seeing your work in print. When I first started, I wrote several stories that were printed in a local journal. It felt great. Start your own newsletter or your own small writing or performing group. It only takes two people to have a performing group, and it only takes one piece of paper and a Xerox machine to make a newsletter.

Are there any quotations you find particularly inspiring?
CMW: I like the quotations from the writer Grace Paley. She said, "Start with what you know and work outward." Most of what you know is your feelings. If I start with what I know, right away ten things will end up on the page that I had no idea I felt. That's exciting. What you know will take you very rapidly into what you don't know. Grace Paley also said that writing is about listening. I don't mean just listening with

your ear. Listen with your pores. Listen to what your feet feel like. Writing is about being a sponge and soaking everything up. It's not about taking it easy. You must be an avid "noticer." You must be very aggressive, and you must notice everything.

FAY WELDON

*F*AY WELDON was born in England and raised in a family of women in New Zealand. Weldon took degrees in economics and psychology from the University of Edinburgh. She has written extensively for film and television (including two episodes of the PBS series "Upstairs, Downstairs"). Among her eighteen novels and short-story collections are *The Life and Loves of a She-Devil* (which became the movie *She-Devil*), *The Hearts and Lives of Men, The Shrapnel Academy, The Heart of the Country* (which won the 1989 *Los Angeles Times* Fiction Award), *The Cloning of Joanna May, Darcy's Utopia, Moon Over Minneapolis,* and *Life Force*. Fay Weldon lives with her husband in London and Somerset. She has four sons.

Why do you write?
FW: I can't help it. I write as I breathe. I started writing because it seemed I had something that needed saying. Fiction seemed a fairly ordinary way of saying it; that is to say, by employing lies and exaggerations. These days I can practically only think if I have a pen in my hand. Yes, I write with a pen. Writing to me remains a kind of ordinary human activity: a manual skill, a part of the brain which is overly developed.

Why did you start writing?
FW: I always earned my living writing. From the day I went to

school and learned to write, that's what I did, though in those days it took the form of passing exams. I responded to words. After college I worked for an advertising agency, which involved market research, as well as copy writing. And I wrote propaganda for the foreign office. Odd jobs and hard times, but all my jobs had to do with writing. I started writing fiction—uncommissioned and unpaid for—when I was about thirty-three.

Did you write in school?
FW: I used my writing skills to pass exams and hide my lack of knowledge.

Did you write poems and short stories?
FW: I wrote only one poem, when I was eighteen. I wrote one short story, when I was fifteen, and when I finished university I wrote one small play. Only when I was in my thirties did I begin writing in any serious sense. After that, I earned a living writing. It is very difficult for young people to write anything which is interesting to other people. It takes time to have a view of the world and to develop a steady personality through which you can see what goes on in the outside world. People can and often will write and write and write when they're young, but to no great purpose. Young people tend to believe that if only they can express themselves, other people will be interested—which of course they're usually not.

At what point do they cross that line?
FW: I think it's much younger now than it used to be. I would say they cross the line at about their mid-twenties. Until then, if a person has any sense, they'll just be concerned with their personal life. I mean with the opposite sex or with the same sex. Somehow that's your function. You should work all that

out and decide who you are and what you are. From that point of decision, you can then begin to communicate with other people. Writing is not an act of self-expression. It is an act of communication. You have to be interested in other people and want to communicate with them, or why should they read you? It is difficult to be interested in other people when you're under twenty-five or thirty. You're quite rightly more interested in yourself, and what could be more interesting? But after awhile, you begin to get bored with yourself, and you start getting interested in other people. Then you begin to accumulate wisdom, and then you begin to try and write.

Do you develop a different kind of ego when you begin to think other people might be interested in what you have to say?
FW: I don't know what determines that. You should be interested in developing a sensitivity that relates to the world of experience you share with other people. There has to be some kind of generalization going on before you can write in a literary sense. You can write a film script or work out a plot, of course, without having to have much wisdom. You can write all that kind of professional stuff from about the age of eighteen. That's not quite what I'm talking about.

How do we encourage the younger generation to write stories that will be commercially appealing but still have a moral and ethical message?
FW: People are interested in what is right and wrong. Even in horror movies, people wonder, "How would I feel if this sort of thing happened to me? What would I think? Would I be brave enough to do this, or would I just scream and run away? How would I behave?" These speculations are what

make films interesting. I think film subjects change when people begin to get bored with them. There comes a point when some experiences, such as horror or whatever, will become laughable, and then things will start winding down again naturally. I think that point will come. I don't think you can dictate what people write. They write what moves them. You can, however, dictate the acceptance of it or otherwise.

What do you think this next generation will write about?
FW: Writers will write about what interests them and their generations. I write screenplays with my son. If I kill someone, I do it with a neat bullet. If he kills someone, blood is splattered all over the wall. I might say something in my English, lady-like fashion such as "Couldn't we chloroform them before we kill them?" He is much more direct.

What is the difference between real life and fictional life?
FW: In real life, things are chaotic, but in fictional society life is about patterns and order and morality. People don't get these things in real life. It's this particular urge to make patterns that makes the difference between a real writer and a writer.

How did you discipline yourself to write when you were raising four children?
FW: It was the necessity of earning the rent. It wasn't a choice, but a necessity.

People perceive that writing is the perfect occupation when you have a family because you can work at home. Is this true?
FW: Yes. It's certainly true. One can only write for three or four hours a day, which gives you the other twenty to live your life, raise the children, and sleep occasionally.

The English magazine She *described you as a curious mixture of a hard-headed realist and an incorrigible romantic. Does that aptly describe you?*
FW: Yes, I think it probably does. I could just say I live in hope. Experience tells you one thing and hope tells you another.

What do you mean by hope?
FW: You hope for happy endings, and you continue to believe there are such things, even though you see very little evidence when you look around.

As a writer, you can create happy endings.
FW: Yes, you can. And you do, and people are glad that you do.

Do you think that's why people read? Is it because they lack a happy ending in their own lives?
FW: I think they read because there is no ending. There's no shape and there's no pattern to life. It's something you do, or something that happens to you. You don't get much of a glimpse of the way you personally fit into any greater scheme of things. You read in order to understand that there is a pattern and to compare yourself and your life with fictional models. Fiction enlightens you with regards to your own life. You balance what you want to get out of whatever it is you're reading. You decide whether it applies to your own life or whether it's about other people's lives. Both viewpoints have advantages. You can move from one to the other within the same book. You can think, "Yes, this is right, this is so. This is how it happens." Or you can think, "Oh, that's how it happens for someone else. How interesting. Thank God it wasn't me."

You confront the weaknesses of men and women in your books. Do you think it takes courage to confront these sensitive issues?
FW: Yes, I do. In a way you do it for other people. Writing can be painful. Occasionally I will read something I wrote and think, "Oh my God, that's true." If it is courage, you're not particularly aware of it at the time.

Do you ever write something, realize it's painful, and then wait to see if you want to go forward?
FW: All the time.

But you push?
FW: You push because it's interesting, and because it seems to you to be the truth at the time. There are other truths as well, and you come across those too. There are good things in addition to the painful things. You come across cheerful and animating things, too, and you think, "That's true. Oh, that's right. Oh, so that's how it is." You might think, "That's nice," and not necessarily, "Oh, how awful." It's about fifty-fifty.

What advice do you give young writers? Are there any specific things you would advise them to do?
FW: There is no right way of doing it. Wanting to do it is the important thing. The other important thing is to distinguish between yourself and what you're doing. What you do is important, and what you are is not important. You should stop thinking about yourself when you write. You think about the story you are writing. You think about the novel or the screenplay you're writing. You try and get it right. Don't worry whether it will reflect credit on you or not. It's difficult for women, especially young women, when they start, because they long to show what they write to other people for approval. They show it to their parents, boyfriends, fathers, or

husbands. Some young women seem to go on needing male approval. Of course that's fatal, because it means you will tailor what you write in order to get approval, and then it won't be honest.

Do you think this concept of needing approval applies to young women more than to young men?
FW: Yes. I find that women ask my advice more often. Some men do, but on the whole, it's the women who want approval. I ask, "Why me? Why don't you just send it to a publisher? Why do you need me as an intermediary?"

Do you think this male confidence is typical in all areas?
FW: It's less than it was. But if a woman submits a manuscript and it gets rejected, she tends to fall away and think, "Oh I should never have tried. I was so presumptuous. I knew I was no good." Whereas if a man gets a rejection slip, he is more likely to go and hit the person who sent it.

Or throw it away.
FW: Yes, or not believe it for a minute. And one wishes women would be more like that.

Do you think this attitude is one of the reasons women have been held back?
FW: Yes, I do. I think it's the need for approval. It's the lack of self-esteem. I believe it was at the University of California at Los Angeles, where this original research was presented: A class of students was given an essay to mark. If the students were told the essay was written by a woman, it received less than fair marks. The women marked it down further than the men. If you gave another group the same essay and said it was written by a man, it would be upgraded, and upgraded more by the women than by the men. It is women's self-esteem

which is at fault and not their judgment. Women seem to have a basic feeling that men's work is worth more than women's work. And unfortunately, women believe this more than men. I'm sure that in some groups of society it's getting better; women do accept themselves as equal. But the notion of being the lesser half is bound to linger in cultures that are strongly paternalistic.

Do you think all women suffer from a lack of self-esteem? Did you?

FW: I wouldn't say that all women suffer from it. I didn't suffer too much because I was brought up in an all-female family. I went to an all-girls school, and I didn't really meet a man until I was nineteen. I sort of thought the world was female. It never occurred to me that you had to have male approval for anything. And when I discovered that the world was run by men, I sensed the injustice of it all. But until then it hadn't occurred to me that when I wrote I had to present myself as anything other than horrid.

What do you mean by that?

FW: When men write something, they want their womenfolk to read it and think how heroic, noble, and good they are. When women write, they want their menfolk to read it and think, "Oh, what a lovely, nice, sweet, gentle, loving creature is writing this lovely piece of sensitive poetry or whatever."

But you said you were horrid?

FW: Let me say I didn't mind being seen, in what I wrote, as horrid, horrible, cynical, bad tempered, suspicious of men, and refusing to acknowledge their nobility or their importance. I was just plain horrid. I declined to take the proper female path.

You took them on.

FW: I didn't know what I was doing. It was a mixture of innocence and ignorance. It didn't occur to me when I began writing that what I was doing was going to cause offense. It was very alarming to find it did. Then I was proved to be right, and everyone else started writing alarmist literature. Now I spend a lot of time defending men. It seems there's been a switch, and it's men's self-esteem we have to worry about. But now women say the kinds of things in print about men, which men would be lynched if they said about women. Now we take liberty to do it. I don't think that's right. It was wrong for men, and it's wrong for women. Granted there is the power relationship in society which still means that men own everything. Up to a point then, you're allowed to be horrible about men. It should, however, come to a more personal and individual level. People should see themselves as individuals first and as a certain gender second.

Both sexes are taking each other on. Men always had confidence, and now women are getting some too.

FW: Women certainly learned very fast.

So you see that changes are happening?

FW: Yes. Everyone learns fast, but not much changes except people's attitudes. In the end, things do shift. I've seen more changes in the States than I've seen here in England.

Do you think the subjects women write about are also changing?

FW: Oh, completely. The domestic interior is no longer very interesting, although marriage remains interesting. I hope we get out. I hope women get out of the home and into the community or into the world and up mountains or down in submarines.

SUSAN GRIFFIN

SUSAN GRIFFIN is a native Californian. She attended San Francisco State University. Griffin is a well-known feminist writer, poet, essayist, lecturer, teacher, playwright, and filmmaker. She is the author of more than twenty books including: *Women and Nature: The Roaring Inside Her* and *Pornography and Silence: Culture's Revenge Against Nature*. *A Chorus of Stones,* her remarkable study of personal denial and how it relates to the causes of war and universal suffering, was nominated for a Pulitzer Prize. Susan Griffin lives in Berkeley, California.

Why do you write?

SG: I've never been able to answer that question, except to say, I write because I like writing. I love writing. I don't write in order to achieve some other thing. I write to write. It's not to say I don't care about achieving other things with my writing. I certainly do. I have a very strong social conscience, and it's very important to put certain experiences into words. Speaking the truth is also very important. It's all of these, but I chose writing as my work because I love doing it.

Do you remember when you were first seized by the desire to write? How old were you?

SG: I was very, very young. I know that I wrote in grammar school, and I've written ever since. I decided to write when I was about fourteen years old.

What were you writing at that time?

SG: Poems and short stories.

The desire to write is often felt at a very young age.
SG: Although it can begin at a young age, writing is one practice that can also be started very late in life.

You talk about keeping a journal in **A Chorus of Stones.** *Do you con-scientiously start a new journal when you go through a transitional peri-od in your life or when you start a new project?*
SG: I probably do it subconsciously to some degree. It matters what I physically write in. I care about the look of the book and the feel of the pen. I don't consider it extraneous.

Is it part of the process?
SG: Yes, it's part of it. It's quite likely that when I start something that feels like a big shift emotionally, I find I just can't put it in the old journal.

You just moved into a new house. Are you going to organize your writing space differently?
SG: A little differently. I've just started using a computer, so that's a change. The whole house was designed around writing, because I've moved in with my partner, and although it's all one house we have separate spaces where we work. I designed one large room to work and live in. I have a desk and a little area table where I can eat. I like to have a lot of space around me. I am also near the win-dows, so I can see the garden. Some people would prefer to be confined to a smaller area, but I like to be in one big space. In my work I often connect things and ideas which were separated before. It's a bit like putting everything together in one room.

You mentioned that you just began using a computer. What method of writing did you use before?
SG: I've always written by hand, and I'll still do that. Instead of transferring my work to the typewriter, however, I'll transfer it to a computer. I stayed away from the computer for many reasons. I had a lot of hesitation. I really like having a computer, but I think

it can be dangerous for people who haven't yet established their own process of writing. The computer can quickly produce material that looks very finished. The real work of crafting is not typing, and it's not getting a page to look neat. It's about making sentences. Sometimes you have to spend a lot of time doing that, and so the slower, physical process makes you really consider things. It is similar to an organic process. Consciousness needs ripening like wine or fruit. It needs a period to come to fullness. To leap from an idea onto the page is not always the best thing. Certain poems can come out very quickly. If you don't get them right on the page immediately, you can lose them. You can't get the idea of a poem and then put it into some other language that is an approximation of your original idea. It just doesn't work. You've got to get the right language. If you have a very good memory, you can memorize it. Occasionally when a line of a poem comes to me, and I'm not able to write it down, I try to memorize it.

It's difficult for a nonwriter to understand a writer's reticence about computers. Writing is a slow process, like sculpting.
SG: A lot of people don't understand that writing is a craft. I was talking with my cabinetmaker, and I said writing is very much like cabinetmaking. You're dealing with something that is real. It's very concrete. It's not suppositional. You're dealing with something that has a will of its own. Language has a will of its own. It has a kind of character that you can only push so far. You have to listen to it. It's not like taking a piece of plastic and molding it any way you want. It's a process of communion or communication between you and the material. You learn from the language. You are your own first reader.

A Chorus of Stones *is at the same time both provocative and yet very disturbing. Why did you write it?*
SG: Again, there's never any one simple reason. When I say

there's no reason, I'm quite serious about that. It's not a way of dodging the question. It's a way of answering it. It's really important for people to understand that creating a book is like having a child. If someone asked, "Why did you have this child?", You could say, "I had this child because I had an empty dining room chair," or "because I wanted someone to carry on the family name." You don't have a single reason for having a child. You have a child out of love, and I think it's the same with a book. A book is also something that is created communally. You have a big hand in it because you're writing it, but it's something that comes out of society and culture too. When I began the book, we were living in a period of time when this civilization was very treacherous. There was a great danger we would destroy ourselves. I wrote the book partly to address that concern and to try and stop it. But the purpose was also simply for the book to exist. For the story to be told. There was something happening in my consciousness at the time—some understanding that was even preverbal about how the private and the public lies affect one another. When I say preverbal, I mean that at the time I couldn't have even told you what the purpose was. I knew there was a connection between the story of my grandmother, who dropped out of the family history, and the denial around nuclear war. I knew there was a connection. I knew they belonged together. In the beginning, I couldn't have even said the connection was denial. But when I put them together there was a kind of electricity. And this was something I wanted to explore. I wanted to know more. As a writer, you're often exploring *with* language. It's a way of knowing more, just as you would get to know a person or a lover. You enter and you know. And it's an act of love, which like all acts of love, involves many dimensions. For example, it involves anguish and anger along with tenderness and compassion, or despair and nerve along with caring.

In this era of such visual bombardment, do you think the written word can still make an impact?

SG: I think so. I love books. I love that medium. It's the word, however, that I think is crucial. I write my poetry to be read aloud. In this culture, we've moved back a little bit into the sounds of words. Rap music is a very exciting possibility. Now kids have the poetry and the magic of words. The thing about writing, or let's be even more elementary and say poetry or storytelling, is that both forms are very inexpensive. They're really a people's art. They're something anyone can do. Babies do it and old people do it. It's a part of everyone's heritage. One of the first things you learn are stories about your family. Storytelling is a very basic human capacity and a tradition in every culture. The written word, however, is not a tradition in every culture. To me, the word is sacred. While writing is the form I've chosen to use in this culture, it's the use of language that is of primary importance. When language gets degraded within a culture, the culture itself gets degraded. When most people think of language being degraded, they think of a lack of education or of poor grammar. But that is not my concern. What troubles me is the empty use of language and the manipulative use of language all around us. And what worries me is *mis*education. This happens a lot through the media. Young people today are just bombarded with images. These images are embedded in an entirely unexamined way. A young person is at the mercy of these nonverbal stories. And there's no way of examining them. Kids are literally mesmerized by this medium they don't know how to operate. They don't know how it's created. It seems so powerful and distant, and kids don't think of it in terms of their own capacity to tell stories, make music, imagine. These images that are larger than life come down at them and tell them how to live. Kids don't think, "Hey what kind of film would I make?" They don't think, "Do I agree or disagree with this?" I worry about computers and films and television, even though I use and enjoy all three of these mediums. The word, both written and also spoken, is an important counterpoint to these mediums that are so expensive and therefore somewhat exclusive and elite.

Why do you think some women degrade other women in films, television, books, and MTV? How can women learn to resist this pressure?
SG: It's very complicated. Perhaps someone who was abused learned that manipulating images gives one a sense of power. In other words, even if one was abused, behind the camera one has power. It is understandable, but in the long run it's harmful to others and it does not really heal the wound. Others may do it for money, or because the pressures in this culture are tremendous. One must resist a certain pornographic picture of women. But if you do resist, you're labeled as being prudish or "uncool." It takes a lot of integrity and strength of character not to participate in degradation or self-degradation. And how does one resist it? I would answer that question in the same way I would answer any question about maintaining integrity in art. That is, the real gift of the art is not the money you get from it, not the fame you get from it, but the work itself. I don't mean to underestimate in any way the need to support artists. We have a crisis in this culture because we don't financially support the arts. Artists cannot live on thin air. But when you devote yourself to your art, without selling out, the gift you receive is priceless. There's a sense of completion and an understanding about why you're alive—an understanding why the earth exists. I couldn't explain to someone what an orange tastes like if they've never tasted an orange. You have to taste the orange. Art is like a taste; it's an immersion in life that opens up experience. Someone who gives that away for any price is getting a very bad deal. For me, writing is a kind of spiritual practice. It's not to say I don't need other things, too. I need fami-

ly. I need friends. I need food. I need clothing. I need all those things. But I also need this work. The feeling I receive from doing it can't be taken away whether or not my work sells. Your ego can take a real battering as a writer, but if you're doing the work you were meant to do, and if you're being true to yourself, then you can handle the criticisms, etc. You develop an inner strength when you do the work with integrity. When you're listening to that inner voice, you can handle almost anything. They call it a gift, and it is a gift. It's not just a gift so you can entertain or impress people. It's a gift that comes directly from the experience itself.

Several of the writers I've interviewed discuss the need women have to try and be nice when they write. Do you agree with this idea?
SG: I would recommend a wonderful essay by Virginia Woolf entitled "Professions for Women." It talks about "killing the angel in the house." You're writing and this angel comes over your shoulder and says, "Shouldn't you be getting someone a cup of tea, or shouldn't you be going out and doing this or that for someone?" Then when you start to write something that's honest, the angel says, "Aren't you going to hurt this person's feelings, or isn't that just a little bit too bold?" You've got to turn around and kill the angel. In popular media today—movies, television—over and over you see images of a hero (or heroine) risking his (or her) life, and killing others. This is a sad sort of substitution for an inner bravery, the bravery which one needs to resist oppression of all kinds. And craft is essential, too. Writing is a craft. And you are taught by the craft you learn. Feelings, insights, understandings, become transformed when you're really writing skillfully. In your desire to create a beautiful work, you move to a larger dimension of your self. A place where you are not alone. And you mustn't put on white gloves and be lady-like. You must take your gloves off, stare, be frank, outrageous, courageous.

HISAYE YAMAMOTO

ISAYE YAMAMOTO was born in Redondo Beach, California. Her parents were Japanese immigrants. In 1942, soon after the Japanese invasion of Pearl Harbor, Yamamoto and her family were interned in the concentration camp at Poston, Arizona. She spent three years in the camp. While at Poston, Yamamoto wrote for its newspaper, the *Poston Chronicle*. She received a John Hay Whitney Foundation Opportunity Fellowship in 1950. Her short story "Yoneko's Earthquake" was published in *Best American Short Stories: 1952*. Her stories have been published in journals, magazines, anthologies, and textbooks. She is the author of *Seventeen Syllables*, a collection of short stories. Yamamoto was the recipient of the 1986 American Book Award for Lifetime Achievement from the Before Columbus Foundation. Yamamoto and her husband, Anthony DeSoto, have five children and two grandchildren.

Why do you write?

HY: I write from compulsion, I suppose, because I've been writing for publication since the age of fourteen, and I am still at it at the age of seventy-two. It's mysterious to me, the whole process of getting an idea and writing it down. It was probably the love of reading that led to my trying to write something myself.

Did it require courage to write, even in the internment camp?

HY: "Writing even in camp" seems to denote some element of courage, but it was perfectly natural (nothing brave about it) under the circumstances. Those of us who fancied ourselves journalists gravitated toward the camp newspaper when we realized we were expected to work. The Poston newspaper was at first called the *Press Bulletin,* and then it became the *Poston Chronicle.* The Camp I editor, (Poston was the only internment center with three camps), Susumu Matsumoto, assigned me to cover several departments such as leave (relocation), law and property, as well as art, theater, music, and library. I also remember writing about agriculture. The editor also had me write a mystery serial, which I called, "Death Rides the Rails to Poston," which appeared in installments as fast as I could write them. I also wrote a personal column called "Small Talk," after a column I used to write for the *Kashu Mainichi,* which was pre-war. After the war, I wrote for the *Los Angeles Tribune,* an African-American weekly, which hired me.

How did internment affect your writing? Was writing a means of venting your anger? Was it helpful to have this means of expression?
HY: More than one critic has remarked that I avoided writing about the camps, and this may have been true, because we *nisei* as a whole were in a state of denial about the experience. There are some nisei, for instance, who never mentioned the subject to their children, who were incredulous when they first learned of it elsewhere. Such parents tended to brush aside questions about it with an, "Oh, that was a long time ago. . ." and similar evasions. I guess my anger did spill over into some of the stories. In one, "The Legend of Miss Sasagawara," I told the story of one person who couldn't adjust to the camps. Anyway, as I look back I see those early days in camp as a nightmare which we gradually realized was actually happening.

How were you able to write and raise five children?
HY: "Not very well," as the comics are wont to say. I didn't do

either, not raising children or writing, with any kind of expertise. During the time the children were being born and growing up, I only wrote about once a year, when Henry Mori, the English section editor of the *Rafu Shimpo,* would ask me for something for the holiday issue of the newspaper. But even one contribution a year since 1953 or so adds up to a pile of writing. For a while I wrote poems, because they were shorter and I could keep them in my head while I was about my chores, and Henry Mori kindly published them. But I understand they were pretty bad. Nobody even mentions them.

Some scholars have said you employ an interplay of opposites in your work. Would you comment on this analysis?
HY: Any technical analysis of my stories puts me in awe that some scholars have found "all that" under the surface of the stories. I write from intuition, and once I get started the people in them start doing all kinds of things. I certainly don't deliberately aim for "this interplay of opposites." It just happens.

Do you believe the written word can still be an effective weapon against racism?
HY: Racism should be countered by all means—visual, written, and spoken. Current statistics about the rising incidence of hate crimes makes a body wonder whether there is any "effective weapon against racism."

Do you have any advice for young writers? Do they have responsibility in the themes or messages they choose to convey?
HY: I doubt that I'm qualified to advise young writers, although I do encourage those with whom I come in contact (including a grandson) who seem to me to have a gift. If they have any responsibility, it's to be true to themselves and to write as honestly as possible. But I must have read that somewhere myself.

SUSAN CHEEVER

SUSAN CHEEVER is the author of five novels: *Looking for Work, A Handsome Man, The Cage, Doctors and Women,* and *Elizabeth Cole.* She is the daughter of the Pulitzer Prize-winning writer John Cheever. Her book about her father, *Home Before Dark,* won several awards. Susan Cheever is also the author of *Treetops: A Family Memoir,* which chronicles her family history. She lives in New York City.

Why do you write?
SC: I don't know. It's so complicated. The answer is the same answer I would have to give about most of the facts of my life: It just happened. I don't want to sound flippant, because it's not a flippant endeavor, but I think most of my life has been a process of letting go of my own ideas about what I should do and allowing something else to happen. Writing is also a process like that. It's a process of intellectual surrender. I decided when I was about fourteen or fifteen that I would not be a writer. It was the last thing I wanted to be. I wasn't sufficiently good at it, and it was painful and futile beyond belief. I did everything I could to keep it from happening. That's the story of my life. If someone had asked me then, "If you end up being a writer, what's the last thing you will ever write about?" I would have said, "My father." And if someone had asked, "If you write about your father, what is the next thing you swear

you would never write about?" I would have said, "My mother." It's the unfolding of a kind of pattern and harmony, which I fight every inch of the way.

It sounds like you don't have any choice in the matter.
SC: I don't seem to have any choice. There is such a thing as free will, and I do have choices, but I *did* end up writing after having sworn I would never write. I became an English teacher, and I was very excited about teaching. I thought it would be my career, and I threw myself into it wholeheartedly. I had planned to get more teaching credentials, but then I got married. I went back to New York University to get a master's in teaching, and then my husband moved to England. I went with him. My husband then moved back to the States and I came with him. I couldn't get a teaching job because of his professional schedule. In those days that is what you did. I thought I had to follow my husband. Now it would be different. At least there would be discussions. In those days there were no discussions. I was happy to follow my husband. And so, at the end of the sixties, I ended up in the suburbs of New York. My husband was trying to write a book, and he wasn't making enough money to support us. I had to get a job, but I couldn't get a teaching job because it was already October. I went from school to school, and I spent about three months trying desperately to get a job. I made macramé belts and sold them to the local ski store. I did whatever I could do. I tried to get a job at the *Reader's Digest,* and I couldn't. I tried to get a job in the public relations department of Continental Can, and I couldn't. I finally got a job on a local newspaper writing the society page. It was the only job I could get. I didn't have a choice. This newspaper turned out to be heaven. It was the *Tarrytown Downtown Daily News.* I was hired to do the society

page, but I ended up doing everything. The first morning I walked in, the editor said, "Someone's got to do the police." So I did the police. The job was about as much fun as I've ever had in my life. It was just great. I didn't think of it as writing, however, because of my vow, remember? I thought of it as journalism. When people would say to me, "Oh, isn't that nice, you're following in your father's footsteps," I would go nuts. But it was a wonderful job. There was a great editor who taught me how to write. I got really excited for the first time in my life. I had been excited about teaching, but this job was even more exciting. I started writing long stories, and that was the beginning. Then my husband moved to San Francisco, and I followed him. I was miserable and I was looking for jobs, with no success. I hated San Francisco. I hated everything. Then I met someone at a party, and I ended up being a stringer for *Newsweek* magazine. I learned more about getting into a story than I ever had before. But I still didn't think it was writing. I came back to New York and my marriage broke up. I was doing freelance magazine work, and although I ended up as a writer for *Newsweek*, I was still saying, "I am not a writer," When *Newsweek* put my father on the cover, they asked me to write something about him. So there I was writing a story about my father.

Then what happened?
SC: I fought it and fought it and fought it, and finally I knew I had to leave *Newsweek*. I knew I wanted to write something that was never going to be edited. The kind of stop-and-start jour-nalism I was doing at *Newsweek* was beginning to make me car sick—if I can stretch that metaphor beyond belief. So I went to the south of France in the winter, lived in a little house, and wrote a novel. I was surprised. I knew I was going to take some

time off to read and recoup, but I really didn't know what was going to happen.

Did you finally feel like a "writer" after you wrote your novel?
SC: Although I'd written a novel, I still didn't think it was a novel. I am so stubborn. I remember writing this 250-page thing and asking, "Is this a novel?" I actually sent it to someone in New York with a letter saying, "Please tell me if this is a novel."

So much for self-confidence.
SC: It was partly about stubbornness and partly about a lack of self-confidence. My friend called me back and said, "Not only is it a novel, but Simon & Schuster just bought it." So I figured I was a writer. I was thirty-five. It was a very mysterious process.

How much of your not wanting to be a writer was tied to your father? Do you think it was a kind of rebellion?
SC: Rebellion is the wrong word. I saw how hard it was.

But your father was so successful.
SC: He wasn't successful when I was growing up. He wasn't successful until the late seventies. Most of my life I watched my father suffer at the hands of editors and publishers. I watched him pinch pennies. I watched him. I knew. It wasn't just the life; I knew what it did to the soul.

How did he feel about his daughter becoming a writer?
SC: He was very polite, but I think he was as upset as I was about it.

Did he try to stop you or at least warn you?
SC: No. By that time I was thirty-five, and I had been writing

secretly in France. There was no stopping me. If I could have been stopped, I would have stopped myself.

Was there any rivalry between you? Was your father afraid you might exceed his success?

SC: I don't think so. I don't think my parents dreamed I would be a writer anymore than I did. I think they dreamed my brother might be a writer, and as a result they put quite a lot of pressure on me not to be a writer. Since they never dreamed in a million years I would do anything except make a marriage, which is what you did in their world, I was pretty free. Plus, my writing and my concerns were so different from my father's. In a way we're the two most different writers on the face of the earth. It's almost bizarre that two people from the same family could have such different sets of interests and such different perceptions. In some ways we're very much alike, but in many ways we're different. My father didn't care about women, and that's really all I care about.

Don't you care about men?

SC: I care about men. I just don't know if I care about men as much as my father did. I believe you shouldn't write unless you can write something that is unique and that only you can write about. In other words, I believe there are too many books already and far too many writers. I'm chagrined I've ended up as one of them, and I feel the only justification for doing this is if I can put something unique on paper. To some extent, the only story I can tell is a woman's story. That's a feeling about writing my father wouldn't have understood at all.

Does it bother you to be associated with your father? Perhaps you would have used a different name if you'd wanted to avoid this connection.

SC: I did use a different name the first time I got married. But the association is not so constant, and I have stopped being irritated by it. I'm fifty years old. It used to irritate me when I was writing about him. I was on a kind of quest to find out who he was.

Are you finally content with being a writer?
SC: It's mighty hard being a writer.

Why is it hard?
SC: It's hard because it exacts such a huge toll. At first I thought it didn't. That's how mysterious it is. At first I thought, all you have to do is do it. When I was writing *The Cage,* I never wrote more than about four hours a day. That shocked and horrified me. I'd go to work about nine o'clock in the morning, and about one o'clock I couldn't work anymore. I thought it was because I was lazy. Someone offered me a teaching job in the afternoon, and I discovered that when I taught in the afternoon, I couldn't write in the morning.

Why?
SC: I don't know, but clearly there is something my writing takes from me that I can't quite quantify.

It's like running the mile. It's exhausting.
SC: Yes, but you also feel exhilarated. It's confusing. I'm extremely confused about the process of writing. I don't know what enables me to do it. I don't know where it comes from when it's good. I don't know where it comes from when it's bad. I don't understand. For example, I'm writing a column for *Newsday.* Sometimes that column takes three days, and sometimes it takes an hour. I can't tell what the difference is.

Writing is not an ordinary job.

SC: Exactly. I learned this from my father, and I also learned it at the newspaper: To do it, all you have to do is do it. It is a great gift to know that. A lot of people think they want to write, but they don't because they're waiting for something. It's like saying you don't want to meet such and such until you've lost twenty pounds. If you want to write a novel, sit down and write the novel. It's like everything else; it's like building a bookcase or walking a mile. If you don't do it now, you're not going to do it. I come at it with a very anti-romantic and anti-sentimental point of view. On the other hand, I don't have a clue how it happens.

Was writing also difficult for your father? Did you observe this struggle when you were growing up, and is it part of your resistance?

SC: My father pretty much treated writing like a job. That was very useful to me. One of the other things I learned from him was that when he had to make money, he wrote. He never said things like, "This isn't quite ready," or "I can't publish this story yet," or "I need to let it mature." He just wrote it. A lot of the things he wrote were for money because he desperately needed money. That's mysterious, too. If writing made any sense, the more time you spent doing it, the better it would be. That's how it is with building a bookcase. But that isn't true with writing. It's so weird.

It is a mystery. All art is a mystery.

SC: There's a lot of mystery in terms of why I'm able to write. I struggle to understand because it is also my livelihood, as it was my father's. I am also supporting two children. There is a tremendous incentive to try and figure out how to make it more like a job. It baffles me.

No one has sufficiently explained creativity. It's a very abstract concept that either works or it doesn't.

SC: I have several stories about this. Someone supposedly once asked the great violinist Pinchas Zukerman about practicing. He practices three hours a day. They asked him, "Isn't it hard to practice your violin three hours a day?" And he replied, "Not at all. The only hard thing is opening the case." There's also a Philip Guston story. He apparently said, "When I start a painting, there are a lot of people in the room. There's my family, my critics, art historians, and friends. As I proceed with the painting, the room empties out. First the critics leave, and then the historians leave, and then my family leaves, and finally I leave the room. That's when the painting begins to happen." That's what I'm saying. My best writing happens when I'm not there.

A psychoanalyst might say it's the difference between the conscious and the subconscious.

SC: It could also be coming from God, or it might be coming from my "disease." It depends on which model of the human psyche you want to use. There's the religious model, and just lately there's the "disease" model, which everyone is using to the max. Writing might be just another addiction. An alcoholic can't tell you why they drink. I'm like the alcoholic who swears off drinking, goes into a bar, orders a sandwich, has a shot of scotch, and wakes up three days later in Omaha, Nebraska. So don't just pin it on Freud.

One common thread I have heard from many of the women I've interviewed, is that they don't have a choice. They must write. Like it or not, they have to do it.

SC: Right. And I wish I could stop.

And take a normal day job?
SC: That's right.

Why do you wish you could stop?
SC: Because it's painful. I know it's a blessing to be able to make a living doing something that comes from my heart instead of working on an assembly line. But in another way, I find it so tremendously difficult. This search for truth—it's very difficult and painful. I have published seven books in ten years, and it's very hard. I don't have fantasies about taking a day job, as about not working at all. I'm not sure I'd be unhappy if I were a ski bum. I'd like to have the MacArthur Foundation finance it.

Are there any joys you receive from writing?
SC: I get wonderful feedback. I get wonderful letters. One of the hard parts about being a writer is having to deal with the editors, agents, and publishing establishment. Once I get through that process, and the book actually gets into the hands of the readers, it's like pure velvet. My readers write letters that show they understand my work and are emboldened by it. It is a joy to know that someone has wandered into a bookstore, picked up your book, read it, and been enlightened by it.

LOUISE ERDRICH

*L*OUISE ERDRICH'S work reflects the magic of her Chippewa Indian heritage. She was raised in North Dakota and attended Dartmouth College. Erdrich's stories have appeared in numerous magazines and have received many prestigious awards. She is also a well-known poet, and her volume of poetry is entitled *Jacklight*. Erdrich's novels include: *Love Medicine, Tracks, The Beet Queen,* and *The Bingo Palace.* She often collaborates with her husband, the author Michael Dorris. Their novel is entitled *The Crown of Columbus.* Erdrich is the editor of *The Best American Short Stories of 1993.* She and Michael Dorris live in New Hampshire. They are the parents of six children.

Why do you write?
LE: I can't help it. Writing is what I do. Of course, I do a great many other things, too, but writing is my work. Everybody works at something. I write.

Did you have fantasies about being a "writer" when you were young? If you did, how is the reality different than these early dreams and expectations?
LE: I always had vague fantasies about being something—I

didn't know *what,* though—and was surprised when writing took hold at the age of nineteen.

How would you define creativity as it relates to writing? How much does one's background influence this process?
LE: We all want to make sense of the world. Stories make sense to me by gathering connections. I suppose because I grew up in a small town and lived in that one place until I was eighteen years old, my feet sank deep in the dirt. My being is bound up with family and where I'm from, and I suppose that I continually return to home ground in order to express, to figure out, to make sense of those overwhelming emotions and events one experiences in childhood but doesn't yet understand.

It must be difficult to find a balance in both work and family with such a busy life. How are you able to discipline yourself to write, while at the same time raising six children?
LE: It was extraordinarily difficult to find time to work while they were very tiny, but now I can work while they are in school. I'm very fortunate in that I'm married to the most resourceful man imaginable, Michael Dorris. Yes, there are conflicts, choices to be made, but for me children and work are a simultaneous love, each life richer for the other. And there is no discipline involved in what you love—not exactly—it is more a form of desire. I spend a great deal of time with them because I want to, as does Michael. Our children are very interesting people.

The wrirings of Native American women are truly inspirational. What can women of all cultures learn from the writing and the history of Native American women?

LE: That Native American women have persisted and survived to this day, to write, to live, is a miracle of endurance and in itself a very great human lesson.

Do you have any particular advice for aspiring writers?
LE: Advice? Love and live.

MELISSA MATHISON

$\mathcal{M}$ELISSA MATHISON was nominated for an Academy Award for her 1982 screenplay *E.T. The Extra-Terrestrial.* This was one of the highest grossing films in history. Her other screen writing credits include *The Black Stallion, The Escape Artist,* and the 1991 ABC miniseries, "Son of the Morning Star." Melissa Mathison is the daughter of the journalist Richard Mathison. She lives in Wyoming with her husband, who is the actor Harrison Ford, and their two children.

Why do you write?
MM: Writing is what I have learned to do.

How did you learn to write?
MM: My father was a writer, so I grew up with it in my house. When I was in school, writing was the easiest way I had of dealing with any difficulties. I could always write something. It worked for me. My first writing job was as a stringer, which is a reporter. A stringer is the lowest-ranking person on the journalistic totem pole. I worked for *Time* and *People* magazines. I had to do the job. I'd get a request to find some information or do a short interview, and it had to be delivered in writing. There was no other way to deliver it. So it became my work. I was trained to work as a writer.

In her interview, Susan Cheever talks about the painful experience of growing up with a father who was a writer. What was the experience like for you?
MM: My father was a journalist. He worked for the *Los Angeles Times* and for *Newsweek* magazine. I remember this image of my father sitting at the dining-room table writing on his typewriter. Because he had five children, he never had the luxury of having an office. While he didn't disappear and wallow in any artistic depression, what was painful, for him, was that he never got to write in the arena he would have liked to have written in. He never had the time or the opportunity. When my father was working, it looked like that; it looked like work.

How much of your decision to become a writer was tied to your father's being a writer?
MM: Nothing that was conscious, but I'm sure everything that was unconscious.

How did you make the transition from magazine writing to screenwriting?
MM: I started working for Francis Ford Coppola as an assistant on *The Godfather, Part II.* I worked on *Apocalypse Now,* and then on *The Black Stallion.* Basically, Coppola sent me off to write the script for *The Black Stallion.* Not knowing any better, I assumed I would be able to do it. I arrived in Canada a few weeks before shooting started, announced myself as the writer and began working with the director.

You just jumped right in?

MM: Again, it was my work. It wasn't something I was able to think or worry about. I just had to do it.

How did writing for magazines prepare you to write screenplays?
MM: I was not afraid of the page. You always hear writers say, "Oh, the blank page." The blank page has never worried me. I know I might have to redo it. I know that half of it, if not all of it, might be terrible, but beginning has never been a problem. I was trained to write to a deadline. If I got a query to do something, it had to be in New York at five o'clock that day. There wasn't any time to sit around and worry about it. I just had to do it. And hopefully, I got a little better each time.

Did that experience teach you discipline?
MM: It taught me discipline and not being afraid to begin. This is what paralyzes most people. I may be afraid to read what I write, but I'm never afraid to begin.

Several of the writers I've interviewed for this book say they don't know why they write; they just do it. They don't have a choice.
MM: Yes. I assume this is what I do in life. I don't have any presumptions to be doing it very well. I just know that this is how I've made my living since I was twenty years old. In some ways it has always been easy for me. In school, I would always take the essay question. I could write my way around things. If I had to do multiple choice questions or something like that, I was in trouble. I've never been afraid to express myself in words on paper. I'm not as good at doing it with my mouth, but I can do it on paper. I can usually get the idea across. This does not indicate

any artistry. It's about not being afraid of the words and the paper and the mechanism of putting it all together.

How did the idea for **E.T.** *come about?*
MM: I was in Tunisia with my husband, Harrison. He was making the first Indiana Jones movie. We were driving all night across the desert with Steven Spielberg. It was a fantastic, mysterious night. Steven asked if I wanted to write a children's movie about a man from outer space, and I said, "Sure." We chatted about it during the drive. So that was it. It was a job. I was asked to do it, and it evolved from there. Several months before this conversation, I had been playing with the idea of writing a children's book with a character named Elliot. I said to Steven, "How about if there's a boy named Elliot in this project?" He said, "Okay, that's fine." When we got home from location, every few days I'd visit Steven and show him what I had been working on. We'd talk about it, and I'd go home and work some more and then come back and show it to Steven. It was a great process, and it was very collaborative. There was a great sense of creation.

Did it surprise you that **E.T.** *was so successful?*
MM: Yes, it did. I thought it was a sweet little movie. It overwhelmed all of us. None of us had any idea. We were quite fond of E.T. We became very sentimental about this little creature. Because of the way the picture was shot, the speed with which it was done, and the kind of nonchalance with which it was done, none of us had a clue as to its success. Not a clue. We wouldn't have been able to work so freely if we'd had any idea in the world that it was going to turn out to be so successful.

Why do you think it was so successful? What chord did it touch with people?

MM: The movie was about emotions. It was about recalled emotions for adults and very real emotions for children. There was something about the community experience of sitting in the movie theater and seeing children and older people laughing and crying at the same time. It became quite a spiritual experience for people.

What projects are you working on now?

MM: I've written a movie about the Dalai Lama that I'm hoping to get made. I'm also going to do an adaptation of a children's book called *Indian in the Cupboard*. It's a great book. I'm working on the outline right now.

What advice do you offer aspiring screenwriters?

MM: I never have any advice for aspiring screenwriters. It's such a bizarre form of writing. I wouldn't advise anyone to aspire to be a screenwriter. I just slipped into it, and I've been lucky. I have written many scripts that have not been turned into movies. It's not a piece of cake. Rather than begin to work in this incredibly structured and lean form, it's a much better route to feel some freedom with your writing first. I would advise people to write in prose first and try to tell stories; or write nonfiction. Screenwriting has become a kind of Olympics or Super Bowl of writing because you can make the most money. To tell you the truth, I don't think there's any other reason why anyone would aspire to it. It's a director's medium. It's really hard on a writer. I've been lucky to have been involved with the productions of the movies I've worked on. Most writers turn in their script, and two years later they see some movie that's dreadful, and they can't stand it. You don't get to retain any control over the script, and everyone and their brother thinks they can fix it. The abuse you have to go through is not the way to begin to write. It's a much better idea to begin to write in a looser form that allows you to find your own style, your own voice, and what you want to write about. If that turns into screenwriting, it's great, but it should never be the first thing you do.

What did you mean when you said screenwriting is a bizarre form?
MM: It is. It's not about writing. It's about visualizing. Your job is to make your description, your character description, your dialogue, and your sequences be as short and as tight as possible. Writing isn't organically about that. Perhaps it compares to trying to write a poem. They're both specific forms with their own rules. Your job is to try and do the best job you can within these rules. Screenwriting is very limiting. I don't think that's the way to begin. While it's something you might wind up doing, it's not writing in the sense of the great novelists or the great short story writers or the great journalists. You're telling a story in pictures. That's what I happen to like about it. It can be very frustrating for people who are more interested in words and in spiraling out stories.

You don't have the freedom?
MM: You don't have the freedom; the space. It's about time. You only have two hours. Whether you have to cover thirty years or twenty-four hours, you have to do it in only two. Although it's very constricting, it's fun. If you're

interested in trying to create pictures that tell stories, and if you find the form challenging, then it's fun.

Have you ever thought about writing a novel?
MM: Oh, sure. Perhaps when my kids are a little older. I have a six-year-old and a three-year-old. It's hard to have any prolonged periods of time when I can work. I've trained myself to work in snippets.

CYNTHIA VOIGT

C YNTHIA VOIGT has written more than fifteen novels for young adults. She won the prestigious Newbery Medal for her book *Dicey's Song.* Her novel *A Solitary Blue* was a Newbery Honor Book. Her other novels include: *Homecoming, Tell Me If the Lovers Are Losers, Building Blocks,* and *The Runner.* She has written two mysteries: *The Vandemark Mummy* and *The Callender Papers,* which won the Edgar Allan Poe Award in 1984. Voigt was the recipient of the 1989 ALAN Award, given by the Assembly on Literature for Adolescents of the National Council of Teachers of English for significant contributions to the field of adolescent literature. She is also the author of an adult novel entitled *Glass Mountain.* Cynthia Voigt lives in Maine with her husband and two children.

Why do you write?
CV: It's what I do. That is to say, if I don't do it the days don't fit as nicely as they should. When people play a sport or dance or do anything they love, it becomes an integral part of their personality. It feels unnatural when they don't do it. So one part of the answer is that I write because it's who I am, and it's what I do. Another part of the answer is that writing is unremittingly interesting. It doesn't get boring. Although it isn't always fun, and it isn't always satisfy-

ing, it's like teaching because it's always new and interesting. The third reason I write is because writing enables me to impose a little order on a world that looks pretty chaotic. When you write, you make your own world, and whether or not it's pleasant, at least you get to feel as if you might be in control. You really aren't in control, of course, but writing is a way of looking at ideas or things that are fearful without having to get in and really immerse yourself. It's a control thing. Control has become such a nasty word. Suppose we call it government. When you write a story about a world, you're governing it; you're controlling and examining it.

And perhaps you're helping it?
CV: At least you're trying out an idea. The world I'm writing about becomes real to me. I can reassure myself that what I think are important virtues are the ones that will be useful. So I write for all of those reasons. I'll probably think of more reasons as I make my sandwich for lunch.

When did you start writing?
CV: I started writing when I was about fourteen. I was in the ninth grade. Although that was the direction my life took, I failed to become a published writer for about twenty-five years.

What do you mean when you say you failed for twenty-five years? Did you send out projects?
CV: Occasionally. I sent things out and they came back. Sometimes they came back with personal rejections, and even that was very satisfying. Many years later, when I was about thirty-seven, I sent out *Homecoming*. It came back with a note that said, "Please, let us see more of this." One of my

favorite stories about myself is that when I left college, I knew two things. I knew I wanted to be a writer. I wasn't sure I'd be able to, and in fact I'd had a lot of negative messages. The other thing I knew was that I didn't want to teach. As it turned out, I was exactly right and exactly wrong.

Did you enjoy the teaching?
CV: The first day I walked into a classroom I loved it. I went into teaching because it was the only way I could support myself and my first husband while he was in school. I sort of fell into it, and it was wonderful. It was one of the best things that ever happened in my life.

What grades did you teach?
CV: I have taught English in almost every grade, from second through twelve, and I've tutored in the grades I haven't taught.

Are you still teaching?
CV: No, I haven't taught for about six years.

Did you get any of the ideas for your novels from teaching?
CV: Yes and no. I got some of my sense of what people and kids are like. When you have a classroom full of people, in an odd way they're intellectually naked in front of you. You can see how minds and spirits and characters work. I know teachers can give themselves away as well, but I never think about that. It would make me a little less spontaneous. Teaching is a good way to get to know people. I've never told the story of one of my students. That would seem intrusive.

Did your students read your books?

CV: My students never talked about them, except for a couple of kids who would tease me and threaten to write their papers about my books.

Did you read books like yours when you were growing up?

CV: I'm fifty-one years old, and I don't remember that there were books like mine. I remember reading one science-fiction novel and some historical fiction. When I taught the fifth grade in the mid-sixties, I found an entire children's section in the library containing novels. Some of the novels were fantasies, and some of them were historical or realistic. Some were funny and some were tragic. There was a whole world that had come into being in the twenty years since I'd left school.

There are so many things to tell kids today. How do you decide what themes to discuss and how deeply to go into them?

CV: What I really want to do is raise questions. You can tell people what to think, but you really shouldn't. Some ideas seem to connect directly with people. Some ideas connect with people of all ages, while some ideas connect with people only at certain ages and stages. I don't give a royal hoot about the question of going too deeply with an issue. I don't think you can go too deeply into good questions. It's disrespectful to my readership to say I can't use sentences with more than three clauses, and I can't write about ideas with more than one level of meaning. Kids are incredibly curious, and they actually give you a hell of a lot more space than adults. Kids are accustomed to learning. They expect more.

What kind of feedback do you get? Do you get hundreds of letters from kids?

CV: I get enough letters to keep me behind in my correspondence. I get feedback from kids as well as from other people. I've received a couple of letters from an eighty-five-year-old woman in Holland. I've been told that people who write for young adults get more feedback than people who write for adults. The best feedback is when kids want to write you a letter. The worst feedback is when the teacher says, "You have to write this letter, and you can't say anything bad." A person once said to me, "Oh, you write for children. I know a child who reads." What a wonderful response. In other words, the person was saying, unless you write for adults you aren't really writing.

How do you feel about that kind of attitude regarding young adult writing?

CV: When someone dismisses what you do because it's not "important," I become a little defensive, and then I doubt myself. Someone once asked me at a literary luncheon, "How does it feel to be in a field dominated by women?" I went into my female defensive mode. Nobody asks the president, "How does it feel to be in a field dominated by men?" When you write for children, you have the opportunity to make a real difference, more so than when you write for adults. And from a purely practical standpoint, my books stay on the market a lot longer than adult books because I'm constantly refueling my readership. It's not the big money, but how much does that matter? I don't know. I've been a teacher for years. You go out to dinner, and someone asks, "What do you do?" When you answer, "I teach," the person gets bored and acts like they know everything about what you do. You get to look up at society from the underside. Although it's an advantage, it's the slave's advantage. It would be nice to punch people in the nose every now and then. They'd pay attention. I have published one adult novel. It did okay. It was called *Glass Mountain*. It was an interesting experience, and it had its own satisfactions. I don't want to get boxed in, in any way. If I could, I'd try and write sonnets and publish a sonnet sequence out of sheer perversity.

Writing for young adults is your art. It's your gift. Isn't that true?
CV: I try not to think about these things too closely because they bring out competitiveness, underlying anxieties, and sexist questions which are only detrimental. There's a murky answer!

Better to just do it, right?
CV: I think so. Take the story you want to tell and tell it, and worry about judging it later.

What advice do you give aspiring writers? You must be asked this question frequently.
CV: I do get asked that question a lot, and I have yet to find an answer. "Keep writing" is certainly a good answer. There are people who think they want to write but don't. There are people who think they want to write because they want to be Stephen King. They want to make a lot of money and have the glamour associated with writing. What a writer really needs are people who will read what you write. You need people who will say more than "Oh, that was good."

You want people to ask, "Why did you do this?" And, "Is that what you wanted to say?" Surround yourself with readers. That's probably better advice than just telling people to write. There is no good advice, and there are no answers. Writing is a very individual process.

YOU, THE WRITER

You've heard the voices of women writers, past and present. You've heard the angst and joy of a writer's life. In each biography from the past and in each interview with the contemporary writers, the struggle to integrate life and art is apparent. How and when these elements come together is the riddle of creativity.

Each writer has a story to tell, and each must embark on a lifetime process of self-discovery. Writers must not only develop their skills and work very hard, they must also put some faith in chance and in the mystery of their gift.

There are endless books, classes, and videos on the subject of writing. You must direct the course of your education and occasionally ask yourself, "Why do I write?", in order to remain focused on the truth. Open yourself to every possibility in life. Be an observer and a participant. Assimilate all the information, hear the stories of others, and ultimately tell your own story.

WRITING FOR YOURSELF

We live in a society that measures success with a dollar sign. This competitive and materialistic spirit in some ways contradicts the very nature of creativity. Obviously, many people write, dance, sing, and paint professionally, but the majority of these individuals would undoubtedly pursue some aspect of their art even if they were paid nothing at all.

When you first discover your creative ability, your craft should be pursued because you love it and not necessarily because you see it as a way to make a living.

Many creative sparks are extinguished when pressure is applied to turn an avocation into a vocation. One of the most destructive side effects of our culture is that as soon as a person exhibits a particular talent, this ability is immediately viewed as a money-maker. Someone may paint well, cook with great expertise, or write inspiring poetry. Why should the gauge of someone's skill be measured by the salability of their gift?

Praise for a creative ability is often a prelude to well-intentioned encouragement. Unfortunately, what is considered the highest praise is often the suggestion that one's craft be turned into a commodity.

Few writers will admit that they are sensitive to criticism. And yet sensitivity and the tendency for self-doubt and self-criticism are very real clichés that describe the artistic temperament.

If a new writer is lured out of the protective and nourishing atmosphere of anonymity and into the professional arena too soon, her fragile talent might be killed by one negative letter from an agent or publisher. Disappointment and frustration can all too easily replace a new writer's drive and enthusiasm. Any outside reinforcement for self-doubt should be avoided until one can gain confidence and a thick skin.

Likewise, if a writer sends out her work and an agent calls her "brilliant," she might feel another form of pressure that can be equally destructive. Praise can be as intimidating and as stifling as criticism. The fear of maintaining the expectations of yourself and others can put an unnatural pressure on one's productivity.

When you're first becoming acquainted with your abilities, there should be only one person in your audience: you. Resist the temptation to share your work with every well-meaning friend who says, "I hear you're writing a novel. Can I read it?" Make sure you're able to handle criticism or praise before you begin admitting the public to your very private show. Once you throw open the doors, it's hard to retreat back inside.

A check from a publishing house may boost your confidence, but it will not necessarily make you a better writer. Many writers rush an agent and send their material off to a publisher long before they're ready. It's important to spend time cultivating your voice and exploring the many possibilities of a writing career.

You can be a doctor, teacher, or forest ranger and still be a writer. Anyone can work in an unrelated field and write as a pleasurable and constructive form of self-expression. If you write simply because you enjoy it, the anxiety many professional writers feel will be removed. By eliminating the stress, you might inadvertently free yourself to write what you truly wish to write about, and therefore enable yourself to dig even deeper into your creative potential.

You can always slip your poem, short story, or novel into an envelope and send it off to a publisher. It only takes one minute to transform yourself into a professional. In the meantime, savor your unique ability and enjoy the act of creating. Don't be pressured into believing you're not a writer unless you sell something. Ignore anyone who says, "You're a writer? Well, what have you sold?" Take control of your creativity. Block out the world and all the intrusive advisers and "experts." If you have questions about where your ability will take you—simply write, and therein you will find the answers.

THE IMPORTANCE OF SOLITUDE

When the Chilean writer Isabel Allende was asked to be interviewed for this book, she declined. Her assistant explained in a letter: "Ms. Allende is not accepting any more engagements. She will need silence to write."

Silence is a precious and essential commodity for a writer. To a nonwriter, it might seem surprising that so many "celebrity" authors are somewhat reclusive. They often decline public appearances and grant very few interviews. One might ask, "Why work so hard to become successful, only to retreat from the benefits of success?"

Many well-known writers spend years cultivating and protecting their very private time. They know what type of structure they need in order to write. In many cases, this is a fragile space and, consequently, they guard it with a passion.

The mechanics of a writer's day-to-day life are balanced with careful consideration. Every writer has different responsibilities and demands on her time. Consequently, one has to learn how to switch gears, shut out the distractions, and get to work.

When you choose a profession that often requires a self-imposed structure, you must juggle all the elements of your life and delegate a portion exclusively for organizing your thoughts. The time spent thinking is just as important as the time spent at the word processor. These quiet, undisturbed moments of thought are vital to the writing process.

Writing is a solitary craft, and a writer needs peace and quiet to sort out ideas, brainstorm, and daydream.

Our lives are filled with stress. Daily life presents countless opportunities for conflict. When high levels of anxiety take over our thoughts, it's almost impossible to be open to the creative energy necessary to write.

Although it's possible to focus your thoughts while working in a busy office or studying in a schoolroom, you also need moments of total silence. If you can't find more than a few minutes during the week, stay home one night of the week. Learn to be alone. Writers must not only develop their technical skills; writers must discipline themselves to do nothing.

A writer needs solitude in order to get in touch with the flow of ideas and allow them to surface. Take a deep breath, close your eyes, and let your imagination roam into areas it seldom travels because of fear, stress, or other negatives that can squelch a writer's spirit.

Taking time for "nothing" can be a very difficult concept for many active, supercharged people. It's hard to accept the notion that productive thinking doesn't just happen. You have to devise a method for switching off your motor and turning on your mind.

You must redefine daydreaming and consider it a positive acitivity. Rather than a waste of time, it's a writer's ally; it's an essential tool. We're conditioned to believe that silence is frightening. In our modern world, "alone" is a state to be avoided.

"Alone" is a writer's sanctuary. You must shut out the world and listen. Become familiar with the process of thought—it's where the work begins.

EDIT, EDIT AND EDIT AGAIN

Not everything you write will be a masterpiece. While some of your work may be worthy of a Nobel Prize, some of it will be garbage, not worthy of the paper it's written on. Great writers such as Jane Austen and Ernest Hemingway undoubtedly had wastebaskets filled with wadded-up rejects.

Many new writers are so pleased they've actually finished something, they're afraid that if they touch it, the piece might fall apart. They're worried that if they fiddle with the words, they'll never be able to get them back to their original state of "perfection."

Objectivity comes with experience. You can almost feel yourself step back from your work and view it from a different perspective. The short story you might consider a masterpiece today, you should pull out and re-read it in a year or two. It's practically guaranteed you'll make some changes.

Unless you employ an editor and critic, you'll have to assume these roles in addition to the role of writer. The ability to detach yourself from your work and be honest is a great asset for any writer. Everyone needs an editor. Very few novels are published verbatim in their first-draft form.

It's difficult to be objective about a piece when the ink is barely dry. When you finish a poem, short story, or chapter of your novel, put it aside for a few days and go back. Much of the art of writing is realized in the rewriting stages. The first draft is often an elaboration upon the shell of an idea, or the filling-in of an outline.

Editing is not only about grammar, sentence structure, and vocabulary. It's about style. Editing will actually help you develop your voice. The more you practice, the more of an accomplished editor you'll become. You'll recognize your unique style, and you'll strengthen your skills as you perfect the language and syntax that is unique to you. You'll be able to take the most boring first-draft sentence and fine-tune it into an original form of expression. This is why writing is called a craft. You sculpt the words that everyone uses (or as an artist uses clay or paint) into a vehicle for your ideas. Editing is an instinct. Listen—you'll hear your voice, and you'll know how to make the words work for you.

Writing is essentially a two-part process. First, there's the passionate explosion of abstract thought, followed by the articulate crafting of ideas into a form or language.

Editing is a game of possibilities. The final paragraph may look nothing like the one you started with. It may be better, or it may be worse. It's like standing back from a painting. You might look at it from many different angles and make a change here or there. When you write, you might take out a word, add a comma, or switch two sentences around. You continue this process until, finally, you stand back and put your pencil down. You know it's right.

Good writing is like a fine piece of silver. The more you polish, the brighter it shines.

PRIVATE PAGES

What is your method for storing thoughts, jotting down ideas, and recording observations? Do you keep a diary, notebook, journal, or just little scraps of paper?

Some writers claim to be inspired by the process of keeping a journal, while others find it to be no use at all.

What is the purpose of keeping a journal? Is this habit a holdover from childhood or a writing class, and does it have value? In this blank volume, you can practice writing, use it as an outlet for your emotions, keep a record of your activities, or use it as a writing log to catch ideas and spontaneous meanderings. By definition, a journal implies that you write something every day. This is perhaps it's greatest value. It doesn't matter what you write, as long as you cover a white space with ink.

The habit of writing in a diary often begins in youth. Many young women receive blank books made to confess their secrets and lock them away. If a person gets hooked on this ritual, they can expand this daily routine into a valuable creative tool.

Writing in a journal is not only relaxing, it's a way of teaching self-discipline. You can write in a formally bound volume that says "journal" or "diary" on the cover, or keep a more spontaneous version that's a simple notebook—a sketchbook for your ideas.

A journal offers the opportunity to be uninhibited and release your "stream of consciousness." A diary, notebook, or journal is very personal. It's intended as a private forum to express the real, uncensored you. Unless you have an eye on future fame or desire a keepsake for posterity, a journal is for your eyes only. It's the ultimate place to take risks. You can say anything, experiment with sentence structure, or let out a verbal tantrum.

Journals don't have to be a record of daily events. Stop writing about what you *do* and start writing about what you *think*. Describe the experience of washing your face, feeling the seat belt against your rib cage, and listening to crisp lettuce crunch against your teeth. Don't just say, "Got dressed, went to work, and had lunch." Get inside life and describe what it feels like. Write character profiles. Describe family, friends, or strangers. Invent exercises that force you to pull words and images out of nowhere.

A journal will also get you into the habit of writing things down when they first pop into your head. Ideas can vanish if you don't write them down. Every writer has a tale about the great idea that got away.

If you decide to keep a journal, use it to your advantage. Doodle, sketch, and make little notes. Have more than one journal. Keep a notebook in your car, next to your bed, in your purse, and on your desk. A notebook is to a writer what a sketchpad is to an artist. Learn to focus on an idea and capture it before it's gone.

DISCIPLINE

Of all the traits necessary to write, discipline emerges as not only the most important, but also the most difficult to master.

Webster's dictionary includes the word "punishment" in its definition of discipline. Although it implies a different context, discipline can indeed mean punishment to those individuals who struggle to be more productive. Why is it easier to resist the need for discipline and give into every available distraction? Discipline is not an enemy. It enables a person to accomplish her goals and eliminate anxiety.

The dictionary also uses the word "self-control" in its definition of discipline. Control is one of the buzzwords of our culture. In the negative sense, one can attempt to force her will on others. To use the term positively, however, one can take charge of one's own actions. Pop psychology encourages people to take control of their lives. For example, if you want to write, do it. Take control.

Discipline enables an individual to exert control over every part of the writing process: The mind, the environment, the equipment, and the time. If you take charge of these factors and dictate an overall plan, these components will work for you.

Discipline is a way of imposing order and taking control of the self. Discipline means not separating who we are from what we want to accomplish. Sometimes these real and unreal parts of the self seem to work against each other. Discipline helps merge one's desires into one's achievements. Discipline is the thorn that serves as a constant reminder: You are the executor of your goals. Only you can make them happen.

Discipline implies a structure for getting things done. There are no magic formulas for adding this crucial trait to your personality. If you want to write, you must push out every possible distraction and admit that writing feels good. It can be more pleasurable than anything else that can drag you away from your work. Discipline may be the prod, but writing is ultimately the reward.

Most writers struggle with beginnings and endings. They search for the perfect punch line and the poignant last sentence that will leave the reader thinking.

There are no morals or witty catch phrases to close a book about writers and writing. The process continues. You will absorb the world in which you live and reinterpret it.

A woman writer today won't have to use a male pseudonym or find her work banished to the back of an obscure anthology in the "token" female section. Women writers are no longer a strange and threatening phenomenon. While equal pay and equal recognition are still goals to be attained, women writers are winning Nobel Prizes and speaking at the inauguration of presidents.

Take advantage of the efforts and accomplishments of the women writers before you. Seize the moment—and write about it.

NOTES

EPIGRAPH

1.Tate, Claudia (editor). *Black Women Writers at Work.* (New York: Continuum, 1983), p. 130.

ON CREATIVITY AND WRITING

1. Buck, Pearl S. *Pearl S. Buck's Nobel Lecture Delivered Before the Swedish Academy at Stockholm, December 12, 1938.* (New York: The John Day Company, 1939), p. 55.
2. Nachmanovitch, Stephen. *Free Play: Improvisation in Life and Art.* (Los Angeles: Jeremy P. Tarcher, Inc., 1990), p. 10.
3. Ibid., p. 73.
4. May, Rollo. *The Courage To Create.* (New York: Bantam, 1976), p. 137.
5. Welty, Eudora. *One Writer's Beginnings.* (Cambridge, MA.: Harvard University Press, 1984), p. 104.

ON WOMEN AND WRITING

1. Woolf, Virginia. *Women and Writing.* (New York: Harcourt, Brace Jovanovich, 1979), p.62.

PEARL S. BUCK:

1. Buck, Pearl S. *A Bridge for Passing.* (New York: The John Day Company, 1961), p. 36.
2. Doyle, Paul A. *Pearl S. Buck. Twayne's United States Authors Series.* (New York: Twayne Publishers, 1965), p. 153.
3. Ibid., p. 125.

ZORA NEALE HURSTON:

1. Hurston, Zora Neale. *Dust Tracks on a Road.* (New York: HarperCollins, 1991), p. 155.

2. Ibid., p. 13.
3. Ibid., p. 107.

GERTRUDE STEIN:

1. Hobhouse, Janet. *Everybody Who Was Anybody.* (New York: G.P. Putnam's Sons, 1975), pp. 175-176.
2. Stein, Gertrude. *Geography and Plays.* (New York: Something Else Press, 1968), p. 187.
3. Toklas, Alice B. *What Is Remembered.* (New York: Holt, Rinehart and Winston, 1963), p. 173.

MARY WOLLSTONECRAFT:

1. Flexner, Eleanor. *Mary Wollstonecraft.* (New York: Coward, McCann & Geoghegan, Inc., 1972), p. 151.
2. Ibid., p. 151.

MOURNING DOVE:

1. Dove, Mourning. *Coyote Stories.* (Lincoln, NE: University of Nebraska Press, 1990), p. 10.
2. Ibid., p. 7.
3. Ibid., p. 5.

MURASAKI SHIKIBU:

1. Bowring, Richard. *Murasaki Shikibu, Her Diary and Poetic Memoirs, A Translation and Study.* (Princeton, NJ: Princeton University Press, 1982), p. 151.
2. Shikibu, Murasaki. *The Tale of Genji.* (New York: The Modern Library, 1960), p. vii.
3. Bowring, pp. 135-137.

FURTHER READING

Bald, Marjory Ameila. *Women Writers of the Nineteenth Century.* New York: Russell & Russell, 1963.

Brande, Dorothea Thompson. *Becoming A Writer.* New York: Harcourt, Brace and Co., 1934.

Chamberlain, Mary. *Conversations Between Women Writers.* London: Virago Press, 1988.

Delany, Sheila. *Writing Woman: Women Writers and Women in Literature: Medieval To Modern.* New York: Schocken Books, 1983.

Ellmann, Mary. *Thinking About Women.* New York: Harcourt, Brace & World, Inc., 1968.

Epel, Naomi. *Writers Dreaming.* New York: Carol Southern Books, 1993.

Friedman, Bonnie. *Writing Past Dark.* New York: HarperCollins, 1993.

Goldberg, Natalie. *Writing Down The Bones: Freeing The Writer Within.* Boston, Mass.: Shambhala Publications, Inc., 1986.

Goulianos, Joan Susan. *By A Woman Writt.* New York: Bobbs-Merrill, 1973.

Green, Rayna. *That's What She Said: Contemporary Poetry and Fiction by Native American Women.* Bloomington, Indiana: Indiana University Press, 1984.

Guppy, Shusha. *Looking Back: A Panoramic View of A Literary Age By The*

Grandes Dames Of European Letters. New York: British-American Publishing, 1991.

Hanscombe, Gillian E. *Writing For Their Lives: The Modernist Woman 1910-1940*. Boston, Mass.: Northeastern University Press, 1988.

Hardwick, Elizabeth. *Seduction and Betrayal: Women and Literature*. New York: Random House, 1974.

Heilbrun, Carolyn G. *Writing: A Woman's Life*. New York: W.W. Norton, 1988.

Hiatt, Mary. *The Way Women Write*. New York: Teacher's College Press, Teacher's College, Columbia University, 1977.

Jelinek, Estelle C. *The Tradition of Women's Autobiography: From Antiquity to the Present*. Boston, Mass.: Twayne Publishers, 1986.

Kelley, Mary. *Private Woman, Public State: Literary Domesticity in the Nineteenth Century*. New York: Oxford University Press, 1984.

Muir, Jane. *Famous Modern American Women Writers*. New York: Dodd, Mead & Co., 1961.

Partnow, Elaine. *The New Quotable Woman*. New York: Meridian, a division of Penguin Books, Ltd., 1993.

Pearlman, Mickey and Henderson, Katherine Usher. *A Voice Of One's Own: Conversations With America's Writing Women*. New York: Houghton Mifflin, 1990.

Russ, Joanna. *How To Suppress Women's Writing*. Austin, Texas: University of Texas Press, 1983.

Safire, William and Leonard, Safir. *Good Advice on Writing*. New York: Simon & Schuster, 1992.

Saxton, Marsha and Florence, Howe. *With Wings: An Anthology of Literature By and About Women With Disabilities.* New York: Feminist Press at the City University of New York, 1987.

Smith, Lucinda Irwin. *Women Who Write.* New York: Julian Messner, 1989.

Spacks, Patricia Ann Meyer. *The Female Imagination.* New York: Alfred A. Knopf, 1975.

Sternburg, Janet. *The Writer on Her Work,* Volumes I & II. New York: W.W. Norton, 1980 & 1991.

Sumrall, Amber Coverdale. *Write To The Heart: Wit & Wisdom of Women Writers.* Freedom, California: The Crossing Press, 1992.

FOR ADDITIONAL READING:
Kaleidoscope, The International Magazine of Literature, Fine Arts and Disability. Kaleidoscope Press, United Disability Services, 326 Locust St., Akron, OH 44302-1876

The author suggests the reader refer to the books listed in the notes and biographies of both past and contemporary writers in this volume.

INDEX